The Modern Language Association of America

Options for Teaching

Joseph Gibaldi, series editor

Film Study in the

Undergraduate Curriculum

edited by

Barry Keith Grant

The Modern Language Association of America
New York   1983

Library of Congress Cataloging in Publication Data
Main entry under title:

Film study in the undergraduate curriculum.

  (Options for teaching ; 5)
  Includes bibliographies.
  1. Moving-pictures—Study and teaching—United States
—Addresses, essays, lectures. I. Grant, Barry Keith,
1947-   . II. Series.
PN1993.8.U5F5 1983   791.43'07'1173   83-8304
ISBN 0-87352-304-0
ISBN 0-87352-305-9 (pbk.)

Published by the Modern Language Association of America
62 Fifth Avenue, New York, New York 10011

Contents

Contents

Introduction

Less than a century old, film history begins in 1895 with the first public showing of the Lumière brothers' films in Le Grand Cafe in Paris. Thus the academic study of film, in comparison to, say, that of literature or painting, has not had adequate time to acquire a firm sense of tradition. From the 1920s through the 1950s, the occasional college course in film was offered—Dudley Andrew points out that the University of Iowa offered film courses during World War I—but these scattered few were of necessity tentative in approach. It was not until Andre Bazin's writings in the late 1940s that the narrow formative aesthetics of Sergei Eisenstein, Rudolf Arnheim, Bela Balazs, and others was challenged to any significant extent. And this was only the beginning of a new intellectual curiosity about the cinema.

In the 1950s, the enthusiasm of *Cahiers du Cinema* for American auteurs, followed by Andrew Sarris' pioneering articles in English (and his regular column in the *Village Voice* a decade later), generated much excitement among Americans seriously interested in film. In his influential work *Hitchcock's Films*, first published in 1965, Robin Wood asserted—a claim that for many amounted to nothing less than heresy—that the films of Alfred Hitchcock were as complex as the plays of William Shakespeare and that they required an equally elaborate exegesis. At the same time, the popularization of Marshall McLuhan's ideas helped cultivate a new awareness of the film as medium.

The 1960s also witnessed both the crumbling of the Hollywood studio system and the critical and commercial success of a number of bold, exciting films by independent feature filmmakers (with a subsequent and inevitable spate of "youth-oriented" movies that seemed to connect with the concerns of the nation's young people as films had not done since World War II). As a result of these developments, American film, for so long dismissed as mere entertainment (if not plain trash), began to be viewed with both an intense personal interest and a new critical attentiveness. And, too, European "art" films, such as those of Ingmar Bergman, Jean-Luc Godard, Federico Fellini, and Michelangelo Antonioni, began appearing more often (at least in urban areas) on American screens. The distaste for the movies voiced by established critics like H. L. Mencken and Edmund Wilson—even by highbrow film critics like Dwight Macdonald and John Simon—seemed now crusty and outdated compared to the rapt enthusiasm of Pauline Kael.

Film culture was thriving by the late 1960s. Within the academic community, film studies were heralded by some as the most promising field in the humanities. Students were of the first television generation, and the swelling of enrollments in film courses testified to their clear interest in the subject. Consequently, film courses sprang into being in colleges across North America. With stable enrollments, healthy budgets, and active student interest in all the humanities, many institutions experienced little difficulty in establishing courses in film, even though such courses may entail considerable expense (film rentals, projection equipment, and staff fees) and administrative problems (timetabling, adequate screening facilities).

In retrospect, however, it seems that the study of film has not fulfilled its promise to become the darling discipline of the 1970s. Of course this is in part the result of the steady decline in humanities enrollments during the last decade, with the marked shift of students in an increasingly difficult economy toward more job-oriented programs in business and the sciences. Yet there are additional factors with which the serious study of cinema has had to contend.

The unfortunate associations of commercialism and cheap (in both senses) entertainment that often characterized the medium in its early days as vaudeville and peep-show attraction continue to do so for some. "Movies" are still regarded by most people more as a social event and emotional diversion than as an intellectual experience. This attitude informs the use of film in their classes by so many heedless, if not simply bored, elementary and high school teachers. Until quite recently, teachers at these levels had not undertaken any study of film and used film merely as a substitute for books and lectures. Since film (with the exception, perhaps, of so many of those awful "educational" documentaries with their pompous "voice-of-God" narration) provides an inherent visual interest, many teachers look to movies to do their jobs for them. Movies instead of teaching, I have discovered in my own screen education classes for teachers, is the way teachers think all too often. It is no coincidence that film use in the public schools increases on Fridays and just before holidays, times when both teachers and students begin thinking more about what will happen after class than of what is going on in it.

Students, in turn, are glad when a film is shown in class because it is, first of all, something different; also, they can assume an easy, passive relation to a movie just as they do in the theater or at home when watching television. Nothing in their experience has taught them how to—indeed, that they must—look critically at a visual text. When these students enter college, they often consider a course in film as "Mickey Mouse" (itself a cinematic term of reference not without its implications), that is, as an easy subject of study. With the greater number of film courses now offered at the college level and with the recent development at some schools of programs in screen education for teachers, this unproductive state of affairs already has begun to change.

Such an uncritical attitude toward film seems even more distressing when one considers the enormous implications of serious film study. We live in a media-saturated culture—a "wired nation" that continues to colonize the "global village"—in which film and television play a large and important role. Studies have shown that many young children spend a large percentage of their time watching television and that by the time they reach high school most young people have devoted more hours to television than they have spent in the classroom. As a result, children are socialized to a large extent through the visual media and do not realize the degree to which their values and behavior patterns have been shaped by the images these media generate. Children in our schools are taught to read but almost never to look. As teachers we owe it to our students to show them how the visual media shape one's perceptions of the world, so that they may think more independently; as concerned individuals we owe it to ourselves to help open the media to the possibility of alternative ideological points of view. These are, to be sure, ethical and political arguments, but they are essential to a serious consideration of what the teaching of film involves and to the informing philosophy of a liberal arts education.

The refusal to take film seriously as a mass medium and as a valid field of critical inquiry is not restricted to the public schools. The common notion among actors in the early part of the century that film acting was a debasement of their art may have disappeared with the rise of Hollywood and the star system, with the lure of fame and fortune, but this view remains essentially that of many elitist intellectuals. It is true (for reasons too complex to discuss here) that film adaptations of great novels have most often produced inferior works of cinema, and for many academics trained in literary analysis, this has been sufficient proof of the medium's inherent inability to achieve aesthetic complexity. Forgetting that great films have been made from mediocre fiction, they consign the study of film to what they consider the more appropriate yet distinctly inferior area of popular culture (if, indeed, they believe *that* vague, questionable field worthy of serious study). As a result of this view of film, and because film incorporates aspects of so many other fields of study (history, psychology, art, architecture, sociology, philosophy, politics, drama, photography), the question of where in the conventional structure of higher education film might or should be taught has become particularly problematic. The essays in this volume by Dudley Andrew, James Michael Welsh, Jerry Wood, Gerald Mast, and Jack Nachbar offer a variety of solutions to this fundamental question.

Two related issues also emerge as major considerations in the serious teaching of film. The first is the question of the text. Because of the nature of the medium, it is impossible without access to special equipment (analytic projectors, moviolas) to engage in a close textual analysis of a film. Thus the teaching of film is immediately suspect for those who value rigorous textual analysis. This problem is addressed in a number of ways by Gerald Mast, Ron Burnett, Bill Nichols, and myself. The second issue is the relation between theory and practice, film analysis and filmmaking, academic and professional training. While the university context, in my view, should not be geared toward the training of Hollywood professionals, the two areas cannot in fact be so easily separated. Just as teachers of literature (English) programs consider writing (whether analytical or creative, itself a problematic distinction) integral to their activity, so the production of images has enormous value in gaining a critical understanding of them. Paul Sharits, Seth Feldman, J. Dudley Andrew, Eugene P. Walz, Beverle Houston, and Marsha Kinder and Chick Strand in their essays consider the importance of "hands-on" experience and how it can be managed even with a minimum of equipment.

By now the study of the cinema has clearly proved itself academically respectable and worthy of administrative support. It is those who resist this idea who should be on the defensive. Much of the groundbreaking work of the newer critical theories and methods—structuralism, semiology, feminism, and Marxism—has taken place in film criticism, often with exciting and productive results. While the expectations for film studies in the 1960s may have failed to materialize, the subject nevertheless has found a place—even if it remains precariously and vaguely defined—in the postsecondary curriculum, and enrollment in film studies has managed, if not to increase, at least to hold its own. According to the American Film Institute's *Guide to College Courses in Film and Television*, published in 1978, courses in film and/or television are offered at no fewer than 1,067 colleges and universities in the United States alone. The guide lists a total of 9,228 courses in film and television, of which 7,015 are at the undergraduate level and 2,133 at the graduate level (the remainder are available for either undergraduate or graduate credit) under the auspices of a wide range of departments (11). Taking into account that the AFI's survey was far from comprehensive, these statistics are quite impressive.

Nevertheless, resistance to the serious study of film within academia remains. This collection of essays, I believe, will help change that and, moreover, aid in defining the position of film studies in the humanities curriculum. After the largely theoretical considerations presented in part 1 of the volume, descriptions of a variety of film programs at both large and small schools are offered in part 2. The interdisciplinary nature of many of these programs suggests a number of flexible models for teaching this most eclectic art. In general, the essays in part 2 progress from program descriptions to addressing problems and considerations frequently encountered in mounting film programs. The essays by Joseph A. Gomez, Robert L. Carringer, Eugene P. Walz, Jerry Wood, and Seth Feldman in particular offer, with the benefit of hindsight, directions for film programs and explain why certain aspects of particular programs failed or succeeded.

Until quite recently, most teachers of film came to the field (and many still do) out of personal interest, having been trained in other areas—most often, literature. The teaching of film has tended, therefore, to take shape primarily as a pragmatic enterprise, and the infrequent literature that has appeared on the pedagogy of film rarely rises above the cant of McLuhanesque "open classroom" optimism. The study of film in higher education, though, seems now to have found a place, and the essays gathered here attest to the seriousness, commitment, and diverse approaches of many of those involved in the discipline. My fervent hope is that this book will serve not only to encourage other teachers and administrators to incorporate the study of film into their curricula but also to stimulate a healthy and necessary self-examination among those who already teach film.

Barry Keith Grant
Brock University

Work Cited

The American Film Institute Guide to College Courses in Film and Television. Ed. Dennis R. Bohnenkamp and Sam L. Grogg, Jr. Princeton: Peterson's Guides, 1978.

PART I

ON TEACHING FILM

Film Study and the University of Chicago

Gerald Mast

Dept. responsible for the film program   Department of English, Committee on General
  Studies in the Humanities, and Committee on Art and Design
Full-time faculty in the dept.   1 (film) 40 (English)
Enrollment policies
    maximum class enrollment (if applicable)   35
    minimum class enrollment   N/A
    average class enrollment   28
Staffing
    % of film courses taught by part-time faculty   0%
    % taught by full-time instructors or lecturers   0%
    % taught by asst., assoc., and full professors   100%
Program size
    # of courses offered in the fall term of 1982   1
    # of courses at all levels offered in the program   4 per year
    # of students enrolled at the institution   3,000 undergraduate
                                                                  5,000 graduate

The film "program" at the University of Chicago is not so much a program as an assumption. The assumption, quite simply, is that films, like poems, novels, plays, philosophical arguments, historical theories, paintings, statues, and musical compositions, are human artistic products and, therefore, can be studied as humanistic texts. Like these other kinds of text, films generate the essential humanistic questions: How are such works structured? What forms, manners, and styles of human creativity do they display? How can we perceive these forms, styles, manners, and characteristics in various representative texts? In what cultures and for what cultures were these texts produced? What do they reveal about these cultures? What kinds of knowledge and tools are required to read these texts as fully and accurately as they deserve? What are the systems of value that differentiate between the greater and lesser of these texts? Although it struck many observers as quite "radical" that the University of Chicago, whose undergraduate theory of education has long been identified with the "great books movement," should devote its time, attention, and money to the study of texts that were not books, film courses at the university merely expand that movement so as to include texts that are not books.

There is, therefore, no film major at the University of Chicago but a series of courses, offered by the Department of English, the Committee on General Studies in the Humanities, and the Committee on Art and Design, that the student can use either to fulfill the requirements for a major in English or general humanities or to fulfill a collegewide requirement in English, humanities, or art and design. Some students enroll in only one or two of these courses, thereby fulfilling one of the principal aims of undergraduate humanistic education—to give the student some additional background, insight, knowledge, or awareness of the procedures of an art or intellectual enterprise that will play a major role in her or his adult recreational life. Other students may take a half dozen of these courses, thereby constructing a sort of minor in film studies in the hope of making a future career related to either the criticism or production of motion pictures.

These courses examine the history, theory, and/or criticism of film (or some combination thereof), an inquiry into the properties and characteristics of films that have already been made rather than into the procedures for making new ones (although there is an inevitable implication that the values of Films Past can shape and influence the making of Films Future—as so many filmmakers of the last twenty years have revealed). There is one course in production. My advice to students (and there are several each year) who want to learn more about making films is quite simple: go make them. Just as the University of Chicago offers few courses in studio art but encourages students who would like to paint to do so as much as possible, so too we offer few courses in "studio film." But each year, paintings are painted and films are filmed, edited, scored, and shown.

The most fundamental course is a two-quarter sequence called, quite simply, "Introduction to Film" (I and II). The first quarter sticks primarily to visual values in the silent film while the second investigates the integration of sight and sound since 1930. Although the title of the course sounds as if it might be found in any number of college catalogs, the course strikes me as unique. For this introductory course is an introduction to the history, theory, and criticism of film. Whereas it would be quite common for a university to offer three separate courses—introductions to film history, to theories of film, and to the principles and terms of film rhetoric (i.e., editing, lighting, composition, camera strategies, the interrelation of visual style and narrative intentions)—this introductory course at the University of Chicago combines all three. At the same time that a student studies the Soviet cinema of the 1920s as a major period of film history, she or he also reads the montage theories of Eisenstein and Pudovkin and studies the principles of composition and editing in their films. To some extent, this kind of course is possible at the University of Chicago because of the assumption about the amount of reading and the number of hours of outside study that each student is expected to do for any course. In addition to two eighty-minute class sessions each week, a ten-week quarter would also require about one thousand pages of reading and thirty hours of viewing outside class time.

With this introductory course as a base, the other offerings move in three directions. There are several courses in specific genres: "Silent Film Comedy," "Sound Film Comedy," "The American Musical: Theater and Film" (which, as its title implies, links stage and screen traditions). There are also courses in theoretical issues: a general one called "Film Theory" and two specific courses devoted to theoretical problems—"Film and Narrative" and "Film and Theater." From time to time a course may be offered in a single major figure: D. W. Griffith, Charles Chaplin, Howard Hawks. Like the introductory course, these courses assume three class hours, three viewing hours, and about one hundred pages of reading each week. Those courses for which there is less available material to read compensate by requiring some six viewing hours outside class each week. I teach most of these courses myself, in a three-year cycle, supplemented by other faculty members in the English department with a special interest in popular culture. The introductory film course is offered most frequently (every other year), the more specialized courses less frequently (every third year).

The eighty-minute class sessions allow the accomplishment of different sorts of educational aims and methods each meeting. Part of the class can be devoted to lectures on essential background material—the historical period, the cultural milieu, pertinent biographical material, the related intellectual issues (either within or outside the field of film per se). Part can be devoted to a general discussion of issues that would parallel such discussions in courses in literature, philosophy, music, or art—narrative structure, the moral implications of the action, photographic style, acting and character, cultural, political, and social implications. Finally, part of the class session (and I think it essential to devote time to this kind of study each meeting) can concern itself with detailed explication of a passage or passages from the film or filmmaker with which that class is concerned. If we are to study a film as carefully as a sonnet, novel, or portrait, it is necessary to be able to study it as closely and as analytically as we can those other kinds of texts.

In film study, this project requires an analytic projector—a specially designed machine that can freeze or reverse the perpetual flow of continuous images so that one can see precisely what elements of style and meaning have been carefully and deliberately built into each one. One must be able to study the contribution of framing, lighting, objects, shapes, motion, color, composition, gesture, music, sound effects, and talk to the comprehensibility and power of each shot. In some shots, particularly those that adopt the Bazinian principle of deep focus and extended take (deep in space, long in time), one must be able to show how intricately and precisely the individual shots have been conceived and, in effect, scored. In other shots, particularly those that adopt the Eisensteinian aesthetic of montage, one must study the precise interrelation of one piece of film to another, not simply their meanings but their graphic and rhythmic relationships. The strongest and most absolute claim about film pedagogy that I wish to make is that no film course can make a serious claim to academic respectability without using such a machine to analyze film passages in this manner (and no film course that uses such a machine can ever fail to enlighten a student in some way or other, regardless of the methods or the abilities of the instructor). Unfortunately, having such a machine inevitably means having three of them, since they break down so often.

This assumption about the necessity of studying film passages in detail has an implication for the kinds of work one expects the student to perform for himself or herself outside class. If it is important to analyze film passages carefully inside class, it is equally important for a student to demonstrate a mastery of these principles and procedures outside class. In every course I require at least one piece of work from a student—either an essay, a question on a take-home exam, or both—that is a detailed explication of a specific passage in a specific film. The implications of this expectation are clear: to perform such an analysis, the university must provide the student texts to study (which means a film library), the means to analyze them (which means flatbed Moviola or Steenbeck viewing tables), and the means to get the films off the shelves and onto the machines properly (which means a staff to serve the students, the films, and the machines).

The idea of a university's providing its academic community with the resources of a film library might seem another radical notion (particularly if radical is seen as synonymous with expensive). But a film library is no different in principle from a record library (which most universities now consider essential) or a collection of newspapers on microfilm and microfiche. Both records and microfilms require special handling and special machines to "read" them, just as films do. There is something ironic (if not scandalous) in the de facto implication of a university library's feeling the compulsion to collect every issue of the *Saturday Evening Post* but no necessity of collecting a single film by Charles Chaplin, Sergei Eisenstein, Jean Renoir, and any number of other masterworks not just of film but of the art and culture of the twentieth century. The effect of such continued neglect at some point in the near future will be the absolute obsolescence and inadequacy of the university library as a repository of the knowledge and culture of the twentieth century.

There are obvious advantages of a film library, both as an adjunct to specific film courses and as the means to make an important contribution to the pedagogical and intellectual life of the university community in general. Not only can students write detailed explications of specific film passages (such close study of a scene or sequence is, of course, as close as the viewer can come to the film's maker, who once scrutinized these pieces of the film in this very way), but the film library also permits another kind of student undertaking. Just as students in a literature class might write an essay on the novels of Hemingway, Dickens, Flaubert, or Tolstoy (because the library provides access to all or most of these novels), students in a film course can write an essay on the films of Griffith, Chaplin, Eisenstein, or Renoir because the film library can make available a sufficient number of these films (not all, to be sure, but many, for a significant number of their films are in the public domain). The existence of a film library makes possible both the detailed explication of a single text and the more general study of a single film-maker, genre, style, or period, simply by making a sufficient sample of relevant texts available for study (and for systematic study, since the student will not be dependent for an essay topic on the screening schedules of the local Bijou or the campus film society).

Another benefit of a film library and study facility is the enrichment of other courses in literature, history, art, or whatever by allowing them to use films that supplement the basic material of those courses. At the University of Chicago, colleagues have used films for courses in Shakespeare, comedy, fiction of the 1930s, expressionism, the New Deal, Japanese literature, and even the introductory courses in French, Italian, methods of literary analysis, and principles of art and design. Although I am the only member of the University of Chicago faculty who teaches film courses specifically, colleagues such as Joel Snyder (photogrpahy), Tom Mapp (art), Edward Rosenheim (literature), Elizabeth Abel (women's studies), Robert Morrissey (French), and Rebecca West and Elissa Weaver (Italian) have all used films for their courses. Further, just as the library collects a large number of books in the hope that individual students or scholars may at some time use them for particular purposes, the film library facility provides the same opportunity for using film texts. Any member of the university community can view any film in the collection for any purpose.

The implications of the last several paragraphs are obvious. It is not sufficient to assume that film texts can be studied analogously to the other humanistic texts that universities traditionally study. Given the specific problems of studying a film text—both inside and outside class, both for undergraduate students and for advanced research—the university must supplement the assumption about film study with the means and materials to study film texts with the same care and closeness, depth and breadth, as one can study those other, printed, humanistic texts. One problem is cost, of course (especially in these times of shrinking budgets and enrollments); a university must be willing to commit itself to an expense of at least $25,000 a year to staff, stock, and maintain a film library and study facility at a modest rate of growth. Another problem is that of the academic attitude toward film—the continuing suspicion that these entertaining commercial products of popular culture are not really worth the serious attention of serious persons (unlike those other entertaining commercial products of popular culture, like Shakespeare's plays and Dickens' novels).

But it is precisely in its overcoming and exposing the prejudices that lie beneath such suspicions that the study of film might be of most benefit to the academic enterprise. The greatness of certain popular films and the popularity of certain great films demonstrate that art need not cut itself off either from the people or from the task of entertaining them to be of value. The popularity of film in this century parallels the popularity of the novel in the last century and a half and the drama in the century and a half before that. The major achievements in film-making suggest the same artistic energy as literary works from those earlier eras when the most significant art was produced not only for the few and was not necessarily difficult to comprehend—as has become the condition of modernist art in this century. The existence of film genres reveals the potential vitality of creating works within a tradition for an audience aware of that tradition; it also leads to speculation about the underlying social attitudes and cultural myths that these generic works distill into the conventions of westerns, musicals, gangster films, detective thrillers, and so on. The study of film necessarily provokes questions about humanistic inquiry and artistic value, unsettling, perhaps, to the solid confidence of literature departments in the accepted "canon" of literary excellence and the principles of taste and value that support that canon. Given the crisis in humanistic education today, that unsettling of values may be a source of healthy stimulation.

It is impossible, however, to provoke or stimulate at all if the study of film is regarded as a sort of academic comic relief—and it cannot be otherwise without the means to teach and study films in as much depth and breadth as literary texts. There is no way to teach a film well if it is shown to a class once, followed (sometimes immediately) by a forty-five-minute general discussion of its themes. Such a pedagogical procedure can only make the study seem as frivolous to students as it does to the faculty; the unfortunate (usually young and untenured) instructor committed to the study of film can only persevere in the honest hope that some kind of film study is better than none at all. (These hopes come tumbling down when the young instructor fails to get tenure because his or her study and pedagogy can be attacked by senior colleagues as being demonstrably frivolous.) Film courses that cost a university nothing, like almost everything that costs nothing, never return much more than nothing on that meager investment. For a university to invest money in the study of film is also to invest in the belief that the enterprise is worth the undertaking. The fact that a "traditional," "conservative" institution like the University of Chicago, whose undergraduate theory of education has long been identified with the great books movement, has been willing to invest its money and its belief in the study of film indicates (however tentatively) that the problems of film study can, must, and eventually will be overcome. Everywhere. Some day.

Recent film courses taught by Gerald Mast at the University of Chicago

English 192: Film Theory   Reading and discussion of the major aesthetic theories that have been developed to explicate the significance and the essence of the cinema as an art, an entertainment, and a system of communication. Among the issues to be considered will be the relationship of cinema to other semiotic systems, the role of cinema in the culture as a whole, and the highest values of cinema as an art. Among the theorists to be read will be Siegfried Kracauer, Rudolf Arnheim, André Bazin, Erwin Panofsky, S. M. Eisenstein, Christian Metz, Umberto Eco, V. F. Perkins, and Stanley Cavell. Appropriate films or passages of films will be screened to test or illuminate the various theories.

English 197: Film and Theater   From its beginning the cinema has carried on a parasitic flirtation with the theater. The cinema camera originally conceived of itself as a single spectator at a play; stage actors, stage directors, stage scripts, and stage values have continually influenced and invaded the movies. Even after freeing itself from domination by the theater and even after establishing itself as a separate art with its own aesthetic laws, the cinema continues to adapt stage works. This course will examine the theoretical and practical problems of adapting a play into a movie. How is it possible to adapt a stage work into cinema without betraying the literary values of the stage work and without betraying the aesthetic values of cinema? What does it mean to betray a stage work or to betray cinema? What are the differing strengths and difficulties of each medium? How can those strengths be translated from one into the other? How can the difficulties be bridged? Students will read theoretical essays on the issue and several plays of which there have been multiple screen versions (such as Gorky's *The Lower Depths* and Shakespeare's *Macbeth*). By seeing and comparing the different cinema treatments of each work, the course will examine the specific kinds of choices that cinema must make and the reasons for those choices.

English 201-1: Introduction to Cinema I   An introduction to the history, theory, and critical analysis of the cinema art. This quarter will concentrate primarily on the silent cinema—the first thirty-five years of cinema, in which film-makers discovered the means to make an exclusively visual medium effectively and coherently communicative. The course and the film screenings will be organized chronologically from the crude beginnings of visual recording with Lumière, to the temporal fantasies of Méliès, to the evolution of narrative with Porter and Griffith, culminating in the first mature cinema work—*The Birth of a Nation*. The course will then investigate the complexity of silent comedy, the contribution of German expressionism, and the refinements of Soviet montage. In addition to investigating the narrative tradition, the course will develop the beginnings of the documentary and experimental traditions in America, Germany, and France. Class discussion will focus not so much on history as on visual analysis, stylistic individuality, and thematic inferences. In addition to the readings in history, theory, and "rhetoric," students will be asked to perform a detailed analysis of a single cinema scene (using an analytic Moviola table) and to perform a stylistic and thematic analysis of a silent film not viewed in class.

English 201-2: Introduction to Cinema II   A continuation of part I, this quarter examines the integration of visual images and the sound track. From the initial clumsiness of the first sound films, the course traces the rapid development of effective sound-cinema styles in America (Lubitsch, von Sternberg) and France (Renoir, Vigo). The course will then examine such topics as individual directorial style (Howard Hawks), the conventions of genres ("screwball" comedy), the differences between American "commercial" films and European "art" films, and the evolution of cinema modernism as demonstrated in films by Bergman, Buñuel, Antonioni, and the experimental work of the Independent American cinema. In addition to readings in history, theory, and "rhetoric," students will perform a detailed analysis of a single scene or device in Orson Welles's *Citizen Kane* (using the analytic Moviola table) and stylistic and thematic analysis of a relevant film seen outside of class. Prerequisite: Introduction to Cinema I.

English 294: Silent Film Comedy   The course is a historical and critical survey of the achievements in physical comedy by the greatest silent-film clowns. Beginning with the comic trick films of Méliès and the jesting pranks of Lumière and Edison, the course examines the specific styles and contributions of Max Linder, Mack Sennett, Hal Roach, Charles Chaplin, Buster Keaton, Harold Lloyd, Harry Langdon, Laurel and Hardy, and such lesser-known figures as Charley Chase, Larry Semon, and Snub Pollard. The course concludes with a consideration of a physical clown of the sound era who adopted and adapted the assumptions of the silent comedians—Jacques Tati. Of particular interest will be the relationship between the creation of the comic persona of the central figure, the kinds of gags he uses to develop that persona, the kinds of comic structures he develops for building whole works, the way that his cinema technique controls our reponses to the character and his world, and the kinds of comments that such a character and such a world make about our own. In addition to the regular class hours, students will be required to view three to six hours of comic films each week.

   English 510: Seminar: Howard Hawks and "Classical Film Narrative"   Study of the major works of Hawks (*Scarface, Twentieth Century, Bringing up Baby, Only Angels Have Wings, His Girl Friday, To Have and Have Not, The Big Sleep, Red River,* and *Rio Bravo*) to determine his themes, style, narrative strategy, view of cinema; these issues necessarily introduce such general problems as the discernment of individual style in an apparent "studio system" and "genre framework"; narrative strategies for adapting popular works of "pulp fiction" into significant movies; do the films reveal a coherent stylistic/aesthetic for the "Hollywood Studio Film"?

*500-level courses are open only to graduate students.

The Practice Of Film Teaching:
Vanier College

Ron Burnett

Dept. responsible for the film program Creative Arts	
Full-time faculty in the dept.	4
Enrollment policies	
average class enrollment	35
Staffing	
% of film courses taught by part-time faculty	10%
% taught by full-time instructors or lecturers	90%
% taught by asst., assoc., and full professors	N/A
Program size	
# of students enrolled in the film program in fall of 1981	560
# of courses offered in the fall term of 1981	16
# of courses at all levels offered in the program	16
# of students enrolled at the institution	6,400

The Vanier College Department of Cinema offers a series of courses within a context that is equivalent to a film school. The department was formed nearly eleven years ago, and each fifteen-week session is made up of between eight and twelve different courses. Although it is not my intention in this short piece to describe the specifics of these courses, I'd like to explain the pedagogical uniqueness of the department and the philosophy of education that guides it.

Its first distinguishing feature is the space that it inhabits. The Cinema Room functions as a combined classroom, workshop, and viewing theater. Tucked away in its corners are editing, sound, and video booths. This multifaceted environment is not designed to be a technological wonderland. On the contrary, an attempt is made to establish a clear balance between theoretical and practical work. Most students and some of the faculty see film teaching and film courses as an initiation into the hardware of the industry. This is the subject of an intense debate. Should theory courses have a practical component? Should workshop courses in production also include some history and theory? Often the rhythm of institutional life tends to sidetrack this debate. The tension that it reveals, however, seems to me to be crucial.

Students arrive at our department with a set of well-defined intentions and intuitions about what they want to learn. For example, in a workshop course they request instruction in narrative continuity. Ironically, in many cases they resist attempts to contextualize and explain the reasons why narrative continuity is an inherent part of only one style of filmmaking. In introductory courses they shy away from and tend to dismiss the application of critical models to their experience of film. They associate criticism with work that they have done in literature and humanities courses. Film, a cultural artifact that they feel they know primarily through television and moviegoing, attracts them as long as its function as entertainment is not too strongly attacked. Obviously there is a convergence between the students' desires as spectators and the need that they feel to be entertained. Unlearning or at least contextualizing those needs should be one of the primary aims of an introductory course. This type of course cannot approach film study through what I like to call the revolving door of a shopping center of ideas. In direct contrast with courses that tend to inventory and catalog the history of film and film theory, our introductory classes try to establish a common ground with students, focusing on the problems of understanding the film-viewing experience. The way that meaning is constructed in the cinema, those elements that give the moment of viewing its particular uniqueness and intensity, is explored through a process of unraveling. We don't so much decode what is on the screen as try to understand what the students have taken from the experience. Why, for example, do they identify very strongly with one character in a fictional film and not with another? What attracts them to, say, James Dean in *Rebel without a Cause* and why do they both dislike and admire his macho opponents? Why do they reject and find boring experiments in cinematic expression, such as the films of Michael Snow? It takes not only preparation but a great deal of discussion and historical explanation to justify to students why Snow's films are important to watch and understand. What, finally, are their expectations about the way that a film should structure its narrative effect? It seems clear that a slow dialectic has to be built between where students are and where the course would like to take them. In the class we end up talking a great deal about stories, how to define them and how to analyse their effects upon us.

Another problem arises at this point. In order to discuss all of the above, an atmosphere has to be created in the classroom that will allow the students to feel at ease with discussing things that are fairly personal in nature. A pedagogical context has to be created within which work can be done on their assumptions about the medium and about the way that they both experience it and desire to create it. In a sense, this method entails the foregrounding of discussions about education, about student and teacher role playing, and about expectations and definitions of what content a film course should have. This creates an initial crisis in the classroom because the students want to see films and find out more about them before they have even grappled with the issue of their own needs. The crisis, however, is a healthy one, because the direction that the course will take is of necessity determined in part by where the students decide that it will go.

The struggle is not an easy one as we go about trying to clarify some of students' assumptions about film and its effects upon them. One of the entry points for this process is the documentary film. Through the news and through television shows like *60 Minutes* and its imitators, the students have become accustomed to seeing the documentary as a "window upon the world." They are rarely conscious of the artifice of the documentary and tend not to see how it constructs a particular point of view. After some discussion they come to understand why the frame around the window is often more important than what is being depicted. We also talk about how what is present on the screen may hide or elide what is absent (like the camera) and the consequences of that for us as viewers. So the documentary film raises questions about the nature of film. The film that I use, Frederick Wiseman's *High School*, brings this out very pointedly. Students are affected in a direct and personal way by the picture of education that they get through the film. I try to explain to them that Wiseman, the director, is giving them a very specific analysis, a carefully crafted set of judgments. Thus the class as a whole has a common basis for discussing what high school meant to them as well as for discussing the way that the film is interpreting the reality of the institution. The conjuncture of education and film has primary importance and forms an integral part of the focus in the early phase of the introductory course.

All of the above is further amplified by discussions of perception and its relationship to the act of viewing a film. Often I will show the students a short film by Stan Brakhage, like *Window, Water, Baby, Moving*. As with the Snow films, they are overwhelmed by the experience. The rules and procedures that they intuitively felt were an absolute part of the cinema are suddenly disrupted. The first reaction is to dismiss the film, to assert that its meaning is vague and unclearly expressed, and thereby, paradoxically, to highlight their own expectations and needs in relation to film viewing. A variety of issues are raised here, including questions about the nature of film language, arguments about whether an unfocused image is legitimate and whether Brakhage's rhythmic panning is meaningful. Even more important are discussions on the avant-garde and the historical reasons for its rise. An entire class is devoted to contextualizing and explaining Brakhage's theories of vision, and these are then placed side by side with what the students feel govern their own perceptual processes. More often than not, they see themselves as receivers of the information that the screen is communicating; as a result, they exteriorize the causes for their own experience, making the film and the filmmaker responsible for the distance or closeness that they may have felt during the viewing. When asked about their rejection of Brakhage they construct a series of complex arguments about the pleasure that has to accompany the viewing of any film. The underlying premise for what they are saying can be summarized as follows: film is naturally a medium of entertainment and in order to be entertained one must lose oneself in the experience, melt the distance between screen and viewer, and consequently be unaware of the structures of meaning that are controlling the viewing. Pleasure grows from this loss of the self.

This essay is not the place to raise questions about scopophilia and voyeurism, but in the classroom I do try to explain why pleasure of this sort must be carefully examined. We talk about fantasy and its relationship to representation, about the careful manipulation that must go into the satisfaction of visual pleasure. An important pedagogical device at this point is the following exercise: I ask the students to bring in a photograph of themselves, preferably at the age of six or seven. We line up all of the photos and talk about the obvious differences between the past and the present, between the image that they had of themselves and the image they now see. We talk about the pleasure that their parents get from seeing the photos. And this then brings up the whole question of the source of that pleasure. Is it in the satisfaction of a memory? What gives the image the power to link memories with each other? What gaps are we filling in as we view the photograph? Most of the students say that the photos do not present them, which then raises the whole question of representation and the image. I could go on. But the purpose of the exercise is to provide a concrete link for the students between pleasure and memory and between viewing and fantasy. It is not too difficult after a while to convince them that there may have been a lot of fantasy invested by the photographer-parent in the taking of the photo and that consequently a photo is not a simple depiction but is a careful articulation, a careful enunciation. Suddenly the notion that pleasure is a careful construction by both the viewer and the maker of a film does not seem too illogical to them. They also begin to realize how much they have to invest to create the pleasure for themselves. It is precisely the ease with which voyeurism allows any viewer to possess the image that the still-photo exercise brings to light.

To provide a counterpoint to all of the above we spend a number of weeks watching Hitchcock films, particularly such early works as *The Thirty-Nine Steps*. We explore a variety of critical techniques for unraveling the meanings of these films, from close textual reading to more general discussions about themes, character development, and the plot mechanisms that underlie the thriller as a genre. Hitchcock was of course also deeply concerned with voyeurism, which he consciously uses as a device within his films as well as the pivot upon which his mysteries unravel.

This process is then disrupted again by a showing of *Weekend* by Jean-Luc Godard. Repetition, narrative rupture, and politics are suddenly introduced into the classroom in a way that is both alienating and exciting. Again the students go through a period of rejection, not only because Godard's film is foreign to them but also because they justifiably feel that it is difficult to analyze and understand. It becomes necessary to contextualize not only Godard but the history of the narrative and fictional movement as it is expressed through the film. They try to understand what Godard is reacting against and what he is attempting to construct, and we begin to talk about the reasons for his choices. In particular, I explain Godard's relationship to Bertolt Brecht and the model of critical and creative practice that Brecht represents. We discuss and delve more deeply into the filmmaker's desire to self-consciously foreground—make visible—artistic, aesthetic, and political points of view, through a medium of expression and through the process of representation. It becomes clear now that the particular form of entertainment that the students have chosen and that they desire has placed them in a position of closure, and for some, this realization significantly changes their perspective on film.

In a sense, the introductory course is taught this way because the object of study, film, needs to be given definition, needs to be defined and redefined constantly. This process of definition allows the students to construct their object of study. It allows them to investigate the field instead of taking it as a given. Most important, in trying to define the way film works and what it is, the students can in a concrete sense determine the direction that the class takes.

The last part of the course concentrates on the representation of women in film. We talk about sexism, objectification, and voyeurism. This is perhaps the most complex section of the entire term. Sexist attitudes cannot be discussed in a vacuum, and it is rare not to see all of the students involved in a series of debates and intense discussions. We now begin to discuss in a systematic sense many of the ideological frameworks that are assumed to be givens in our culture.

At this point the students are also encouraged to make a film. Since it is usually the first film for most of them, the guidelines that they are given are general in nature. However, a strong suggestion is made that they try to create as personal a film as possible. They are helped in this process by a series of half-hour workshops conducted by the technician who works in the Cinema Room. In general, they use Super-8, which allows them to work individually. Sometimes a few of the more adventurous students will group together and work with video. The films that the students make are heterogeneous in nature, but inevitably, because they are very personal, they reveal a great deal about the individuals who make them. And here the connection is made with the ongoing discussions that we are having in the classroom about the objectification of the female body in most media. It becomes clear that the creative act is deeply bound up with the attitudes that we hold. Those attitudes act as filters, defining, often unconsciously, the choices that are being made in the attempt to structure a meaningful statement through film. These same filters act on us as viewers, and the students are now able to link the problems of creativity with those of interpretation. The last two weeks of the term are entirely devoted to the screening of their films. Their grades are arrived at through a personal interview and discussion of their work and their participation in the class discussions. Those students who haven't made a film or participated to any degree are required to write a paper on one of the ideas explored in the course.

Though the students enter the course with the desire for it to be technical in nature, that desire is confronted and then contextualized. This is perhaps the most important facet of the teaching that is done in the cinema department at Vanier College. It is crucial not to separate theory from practice. It would be a mistake, particularly in the study of film, to make that separation a fundamental part of the curriculum. Film courses should reflect the stresses and strains of film theory (which is evolving and changing at all times) and should also reflect and reflect upon the work that a variety of different filmmakers are creating, from the experimental to the most traditional. What must be avoided, it seems to me, is the tendency to make film courses a simple catalog of techniques and styles, an exploration of the formal history of the medium without a concurrent explanation of the theory that has given rise to that formalism. If the relationship between a film and an audience were a direct and unmediated one—unmediated, that is, by the theater environment, the screen texture, the type of audience, the class position of the viewer, and so on—then film's effects would be understood and film would be a utopia for the filmmaker, a place where the meaning of the objects and subjects on the screen would be immediately understood by direct transference to consciousness. But the viewers of a film see many different things, and it is precisely because of this that the ideological intent and framework of the film have to be understood and challenged. Between the spaces created by what is said and by what is understood lie the possibilities for the transformation of how we approach our comprehension of film. For it becomes clear, then, that film is not solely a means of communication but is also a sort of mythic noisemaker. If there is any myth that students need to be taught about in relation to film, if there is any myth that needs to be unmasked, it is that the sound and images emanating from the screen affect the viewer in a total way without any participation by the viewer. This undialectical but central notion imputes a power to the medium that it cannot have, unless those watching it are not using what is presented to help construct an experience. It is this type of objectification that sustains the status of film as an experience different from and more special than any other. By making it appear as if the audience is not aiding in the construction of what it is seeing (in a dialectical fashion), the perceptual and cognitive activity of each viewer is obscured, and what we are left with is "magic." But that notion of magic is a carefully constructed myth that viewers bring to the theater. It allows them to deny to themselves the work they are doing to make the experience happen. This is why teaching film is such a delicate task. It must be approached with a knowledge of the preconceptions that the students bring to the classroom and with ideas for how to challenge and contextualize them. This is perhaps the most important contribution that the Vanier College cinema department has made to the study and teaching of film.

Vanier College

Vanier College is a College of General and Professional Education (CEGEP) located on two campuses in the western part of Montreal. The college was established in 1970 when the Quebec Government agreed to open a second English-language CEGEP. Since 1970 the college has grown steadily, until today there are six thousand students and over four hundred faculty located at two campuses. The first campus was established in Saint Laurent and now has about four thousand students. The other campus was opened in 1973 in the Snowdon district and has grown to two thousand students.

Department of Cinema

The cinema department offers a wide range of courses in practical and theoretical aspects of filmmaking, in communications, and in film study. Courses like "Modern Cinema," "Journalism," "Mass Media and Communications," "The Film," and "Quebec Cinema" are designed to stimulate an interest in learning how to interpret communications phenomena using different strategies and to help develop an understanding of media in their social context. Psychological, aesthetic, sociological, and historical approaches to communications are explored with a view toward understanding their strengths and limitations. The workshop courses emphasize participatory learning, practice with the technology through exercises, and intensive feedback sessions on student-initiated projects.

All cinema courses described are open to all students in careers, arts, or science programs. For those students who wish to specialize in cinema or communications, the department offers a program of concentration in either area. Both concentrations are given with the Creative Arts D.E.C. ("Diplôme des Etudes Collégiales").

Cinema Concentration

1st semester:	950 and 902 (2)
2nd semester:	910 or 911 or 912 (1)
3rd semester:	951 and/or 940 or 942 (1 or 2)
4th semester:	930 or 943 or departmental seminar (1 or 2)
	(Total of 6)

Communications Concentration

1st semester:	901 and 942 (2)
2nd semester:	950 (1)
3rd semester:	941 and/or 943 (1 or 2)
4th semester:	Departmental seminar and/or 951 (1 or 2)
	(Total of 6)

Also, apart from regular courses, the cinema and communications department offers several intensive workshops and seminars bearing on various aspects of film study and communication theory (e.g., workshops on Godard, Hitchcock, Scorsese, women and film; seminar on psychological and cultural aspects of audiovisual communication).

Courses

901: Cinema and Society: Introduction to Media Production   This course will involve study of the media of film, photography, and television and the different stylistic techniques used for each type of message a society sees as useful, entertaining, and informative. Students will be urged to work with these media to explore various forms of media production as well as to create their own. Modern technology has allowed for image and sound recording to be used in a wide variety of contexts, to communicate about an almost unlimited number and type of events. In this technology, audiovisual media are expected to be properly operated to generate the effect or information desired. What, then, are the differences in technique and style necessary when filming or photographing a person for the news, for a portrait, a feature film, a passport, or an advertisement? How do such technical details affect or change the meaning of images and the object or event the images represent?

902: Introduction to Film   This course is an introduction to ways of studying film. During class a wide variety of Hollywood, experimental, and political films will be screened, to be followed by group discussions. Talking about the films we see will give us an opportunity to understand the ways in which people relate to films and the strategies they use to interpret them. We can then start to question the basis and nature of this relationship and develop ways of becoming more critical and more sensitive to the different levels through which film can be interpreted.

910: *History of Film*   This course examines the origins and growth of the movie business from the beginnings in the early 1890s down to the present day. The "background" part of the course will focus on key developments in film technology, film aesthetics, themes, and the film business. The course will consist of classroom presentations, readings on the growth of the movies, and screenings of important films.

911: *Film Genres and Directors*   Every semester this course will focus on the films of a particular genre or film director. We will examine the validity of genre and auteur study as a way of criticizing and studying film and then proceed to an exploration of the cinematic codes that define a particular genre or director. We shall also discuss the social and economic context in which a genre is produced and that in turn influences it.

912: *Modern Cinema*   The modern cinema is a revolt against a particular style of filmmaking with its own conventions: characterization, narrative tradition, etc. Here we will examine the character of these developments in comparison with the established traditions and conventions in cinema.

922: *Quebec Cinema*   This course explores the complexities—social, political, historical—of Quebec cinema and culture. We will examine how films made in Quebec reflect the problems, values, and contradictions of this society. We will learn how to "situate" film within its social context.

930: *Modes of Film Analysis*   Taking the contributions of critics into account, the course will attempt to generate its own responses to specific films. Students will therefore be dealing with both the nature of the film and the means by which a film can be placed within the framework of our social experiences. The topics and films will vary, although some emphasis will be given to modernist and experimental films that challenge our ways of seeing and understanding. Classes will depend heavily on student presentations and discussions. Prerequisite: one cinema course recommended.

940: *Writing and Film*   A workshop course for students interested in exploring the idea of writing in relation to film and tv. The focus of the course will be on developing students' own "writing" and on learning how to translate students' own vision into the most appropriate forms of "script." During class, various genres and styles will be screened and discussed in terms of their dramatic structure, characterization, and dialogue. Classes will depend heavily on student input and participation.

941: *Origins and Foundations of Mass Communications*   An extensive inquiry into the idea of mass communications and their intended function. The course will be divided into three themes: social or macroscopic, personal or microscopic, and the relation between the two. Prerequisite: one cinema course recommended.

942: *Mass Media and Communications*   How do media of communication influence the process of cultural and political change? To what extent are we shaping and being shaped by these powerful institutions that are responsible for defining social reality? Media covered include television, newspapers, radio, and film.

943: Journalism and the Documentary Film   This course is designed to allow students an opportunity to learn about journalism in the mass media (television, radio, film) by participating in creative exercises and group discussions. Documentary techniques influence the ways we think about processes of change in our social systems. How is a news report constructed for television? Are documentaries really different from fictional films? Can film and video be used as tools for community action? In order to answer these questions we shall make films, look at the traditions of journalism in film and television, and talk to people active in the field. This will involve a flexible approach to learning, emphasizing student participation in the definition of goals and activities.

950: Cinematography I   This is not a course in the technique of filmmaking; it is a course on how to develop the creative impulses within the student. The course is an open-ended workshop.

951: Cinematography II   This course will deal with problems of creative expression in film by examining the relationships between film theory and filmmaking. We shall try to answer the following question: How does a student's understanding of film (aesthetic, political, etc.) affect the ways in which he or she makes films? In order to answer this question we shall look at different styles of film—documentary, commercial, experimental, and political—and try to discover the theories about film that underlie the different styles. At the same time that we are looking at films we shall be making them together inside and outside of class. Prerequisite: 950.

Notes on Experience and the Teaching of Film: Brock University

Barry Keith Grant

Dept. responsible for the film program	Fine Arts	
Full-time faculty in the dept.		12
Enrollment policies		
maximum class enrollment (if applicable)		N/A
minimum class enrollment		10
average class enrollment		20
Staffing		
% of film courses taught by part-time faculty		10%
% taught by full-time instructors or lecturers		20%
% taught by asst., assoc., and full professors		70%
Program size		
# of students enrolled in the film program in fall of 1982		15
# of courses offered in the fall term of 1982		7
# of courses at all levels offered in the program		13
# of students enrolled at the institution		3,500

One of the primary issues in the teaching of film, as indeed in teaching any other subject, is, as Leslie Fiedler puts it, "What can, and what should, be taught?" And whether one considers Fiedler's ruminations on that question to be somewhat cynical—he insists that because teaching is "a passion, not a science . . . methods therefore are meaningless in the classroom"—his conclusion remains fundamentally true: "Once we have realized that the teacher is not just a guide, much less a substitute parent or a charming entertainer (though he can be all of these things as well), but a model," we will understand "that what is learned in the classroom is him, the teacher" (273, 275). From personal experience I would agree that what is, although not necessarily taught, nevertheless learned by students—especially lower-level students—is the teacher himself or herself, as role model either positive or negative.

Freshman are entering a new environment, one of living as well as learning, that grants them more freedom, space, and responsibility than they have known previously. It is likely to seem to them alternately attractive and threatening. And it is also likely that in such circumstances (not unlike the classic therapy situation) they will not only consider the teacher they respect as an authority but also seek to identify with and emulate him or her. In the highly charged dynamic of the classroom students are easily able to spot teachers who are generally indifferent or hostile to their subjects. This is the kind of teacher students can never respect; in such instances students tend to respond to the material in a similarly uninspired fashion. Conversely, teachers truly excited by and interested in what they are teaching are more apt to have animated and interested students in their classes. If students respect the instructor, they are inclined to respect his or her object of instruction.

There have been times when I have been aware, as I was lecturing to my "Introduction to Film Criticism" class (usually between fifty and sixty students), that students were paying only the slightest attention to what I was saying; rather, they were studying me and the manner in which I rambled on about the semiotic codes in *Stagecoach* or the cultural forces that converged to form the style of *film noir*. Certainly it is possible to view this state of affairs as nothing more than an unfortunate cult of personality. But I would like to suggest that the most effective teachers, particularly at the first-year level, are the ones who accept this situation as a given and, further, are willing to exploit it by incorporating it into their teaching styles. In its simplest form what I'm suggesting amounts to little more than saying that if teachers do not demonstrate an enthusiasm for their subjects, obviously their students won't either. No one, I think, would disagree with that. But I mean to imply something more: that if teachers reveal to their students what the material has meant for them—their aesthetic biography, so to speak—then students are more apt to see the relevance of the stuff and hence become more genuinely interested in studying it. What I would like to do now, then, is explain how I have tried to combine these observations with both my aesthetic ideas and pedagogical practice concerning film.

Much academic suspicion about the teaching of film is based on the ephemeral nature of the cinematic text. How can rigorous analytical discussion of film take place in the classroom when in most cases neither teachers nor students are able to have the text in front of them? Except where special equipment is available, students are forced to rely on memory. Moreover, it is likely that they will have seen the film to be discussed only once, which means they will not have been able to divorce themselves completely from emotional involvement with the narrative and characters. Such discussion, it would seem, must therefore degenerate into mere impressionism and subjective assertion.

It is true that students will tend to respond to films in basic emotional ways, even to the films by Eisenstein, Rossellini, and other formal innovators outside the Hollywood mainstream that they are likely to encounter in an introductory course. Yet this is only congruent with their experience of film outside the classroom. More than literature or the theater the visual media today constitute an aesthetic tradition that is truly lived by most people. Both tv and film are commonly and above all else social events, like the drama used to be. People gather around the family tv set, prominently placed in the living room, as if it were a technological hearth; they are mutually suckled by the warm glow of the appropriately named boob tube, whether at home or in a tavern. The Academy Awards ceremony is an annual ritual watched and discussed by millions, while the National Book Awards receive hardly the same degree of media coverage. This is not to imply the superiority of cinema to literature but simply to state the manner in which the two forms function in our society. Few couples go out on dates to the local library, after all. Whether it is true or not, one periodically hears arguments about the death of the novel or of the theater. The visual media, by contrast, are anything but dead, and no one, with the possible exception of pessimistic Hollywood producers and optimistic video-disc technocrats, has announced the passing of the movies as a major cultural force.

Brock University, located in Ontario's Niagara Peninsula, is not much different from most smaller North American universities. Its 3,500 students have gravitated toward the sciences and business administration, while humanities enrollments have slowly but steadily declined. Most first-year humanities courses are now taken to fulfill the university's degree requirements. Each year, more than half the students who enroll in the "Introduction to Film Criticism" course admit or inadvertently betray that they did so initially because they thought it would be an easy credit. Cultural experience has taught them that whereas literature is art to be analyzed, movies are entertainment to be enjoyed. Consequently, students are consistently more defensive and resistant in beginning film courses than they are in literature courses. Always I am asked, often with great urgency, if the course will destroy their ability to escape passively into movies. Yet in a fundamental way this predictable response can be exploited, can become an asset to the teacher of film. Simply to say anything intelligent about a commercial movie beyond the personal response of "I liked it" or "I didn't" is likely to amaze many students. And amazement, like the "sense of wonder" so dear to the defenders of science fiction, can act as a psychic crowbar to prize open new avenues of inquiry for even moderately receptive minds.

For some years now I have been interested in the aesthetic approach termed contextualism by Stephen C. Pepper, an aesthetic grounded in the notion of art as experience. For the contextualist the aesthetic experience constitutes the vital interaction between the physical work of art and the spectator. In this sense, the phrase "work of art" implies an action rather than an object; as John Dewey puts it in *Art as Experience* (for Pepper the central work of contextualist aesthetics): "Art is the quality of doing and of what is done. Only outwardly, then, can it be designated by a noun substantive. . . . The *product* of art—temple, painting, statue, poem—is not the *work* of art. The work takes place when a human being cooperates with the product so that the outcome is an experience that is enjoyed because of its liberating and ordered properties" (214). The specific nature or "quality" of this experience—what Pepper called "the character, the mood, and you might almost say, the personality" (59) of the event—becomes the central subject of inquiry for the contextualist, who, therefore, ultimately must consider both the physical work of art and his or her own responses in making aesthetic judgments.

Contextualism clearly offers a particularly relevant approach to the teaching of film at the introductory level. As the semiotician Christian Metz has remarked, the cinema is "the 'phenomenological' art *par excellence*" (43); and while phenomenological criticism tends to treat consciousness more discretely than contextualism, Metz's assertion reveals the extent to which film engages the viewer. This engagement is basically twofold. First, cinema is more than any other medium an art of illusion, for the perception of a motion picture begins with the "synthesis" by the spectator's eye of the individual still frames; and second, the viewer's willing suspension of disbelief is particularly strong in the cinema, where it is encouraged by images and sounds larger and louder than life. (Thus, film's apparent affinity for the melodramatic, the fantastic, and the spectacular—narrative modes that tend to magnify or exaggerate reality—does not necessarily constitute "inferior" cinema and is actually quite natural.) It is no accident that the cinema's greatest artists consistently have been concerned with this central fact of the film experience. The films of primarily "emotional" directors, such as Hitchcock, Chabrol, or Truffaut, for example, depend upon audience expectations, identification, and involvement, just as more intellectual filmmakers, like Eisenstein, Godard, and Fassbinder, structure their work according to their respective theories of audience involvement and its implications. Even the "closed" cinema of Fritz Lang derives both its power and meaning from audience involvement as much as the "open" cinema of Jean Renoir—the former by encouraging judgments in the viewer subsequently exposed as corrupt; the latter, oppositely, by inviting suspension of judgment. (The extremely helpful concept of open and closed styles is explored by Leo Braudy in *The World in a Frame*.) Still other directors—Buñuel, Fellini, Cocteau—exploit the cinema's special contiguity with various levels of experience (dreams, fantasy). Their film practice is in agreement with Suzanne Langer's observation that "cinema is 'like' dream in the mode of its presentation: it creates a virtual present, an order of direct apparition" (412). Yet whether these directors consider emotional or intellectual involvement of paramount importance, they all begin with the basic and necessary fact of viewer interaction.

Now, aside from their naive propensity for amazement, the main thing beginning students in film bring to class is their experience of the film they have seen that week. Despite their resistance to analyzing films, they tend to be more willing to discuss their responses since film has a relatively lowbrow cultural status as compared to literature. What I try to do first is get the students to articulate their responses to the film and then, going back to the film in their memory, try to decide whether it was working in such a way as to elicit this response, or if their experience was brought to the film by stock responses or their own personal connotations. If we agree that a particular instance falls into the latter category, I explain why it is irrelevant to an understanding of the film itself; if, on the other hand, their response seems an example of the former, the next question we consider is whether or not the film had created that experience or response in them as part of a larger design or thematic structure. This seems to me a practical way of demonstrating the separate but not necessarily mutually exclusive realms of taste and criticism.

A couple of examples will serve to make this procedure clear. The first film I usually screen in the introductory course is Alfred Hitchcock's *Psycho* (1960). I choose this film to begin the course because it was and still is a popular film that also has some quite serious things to say; in other words, it is at once accessible and artistic. And, of course, it always produces strong responses in its audience. I use this film first to provide a general procedural model for the rest of the course by doing a shot analysis in which I discuss camera movement, movement within the frame, lighting, editing, and so on, showing how to discern these elements and then considering how they function meaningfully in context. *Psycho* also provides a useful example for pointing out the difference between exploitation horror films and aesthetically valid ones. Students assume it is their strong reaction to a horror film that makes it good, but this is not necessaily the case. I explain that it is actually not very difficult for a film to scare us, pointing out such worn devices as a hand suddenly appearing in the frame in a tight close-up—a technique that is usually as effective as it is common, yet as creaky as the old house in which it often occurs. The good film, however, will elicit fear (or whatever the emotion may be) in a meaningful way, say, to clarify the experience of fear. Pepper goes so far as to declare that from the contextualist point of view the best works are those that intensify and clarify experience, either of the work itself or beyond it. The pleasure of experience, while not disregarded, is secondary to its force: "*The more vivid the aesthetic experience and the more extensive and rich its quality,*" he states, "*the greater its aesthetic value*" (57, italics in the original). And as a genre the horror film lends itself readily to contextualist analysis, for the raison d'être of these films is to elicit vivid aesthetic response.

What makes *Psycho* a work of some profundity and depth and not merely a cheap shocker is that Hitchcock manages in his stylistic treatment of the narrative to implicate the viewers morally in the events they are watching on the screen, thus connecting the experience of viewing the film with the actions of the characters in the film. As a result, we are forced to confront the characters' impurities as our own. Or so the argument goes. This is not the place to elaborate on this fundamental thrust of Hitchcock criticism—the best place to begin is with Robin Wood's *Hitchcock's Films*—but rather, to illustrate how such ideas may be incorporated into the practice of teaching. For me, one of the most significant moments in the film comes during the scene in which Norman Bates (Anthony Perkins) sinks the automobile with the body of Marion Crane (Janet Leigh) in the trunk into the swamp behind the motel: the car stops for a moment, as if the swamp is too shallow to accommodate it, and then, after this slight pause, it abruptly bubbles and continues to sink as suddenly as it stopped. This scene occurs after Norman's elaborate cleanup of his mother's mess in Marion's room (Hitchcock pans to the newspaper with the money folded within, a fact we know but Norman doesn't), a sequence that encourages viewers to switch their identification to and sympathy for Norman from the now dead Marion. Every time I see the car-sinking scene I notice an audible, almost palpable, sigh of relief in the audience as the car renews its watery descent. After discussion about how they felt at this moment in the film, students remember that sigh of relief or an equivalent feeling. Because they have experienced it rather than simply been told about it, they understand more fully the critical argument concerning Hitchcock advanced by Wood and others. They know that because they responded that way they have been implicated in the fantasy of the perfect crime—a fantasy that in part drives Marion to her crime in the first place. It is all the difference between a thesis and a demonstration, in Dewey's terms between a product of art and a work of art.

My second example concerns *Written on the Wind* (1956), directed by Douglas Sirk, also a maker of popular Hollywood films but one who worked in a more subtle manner than Hitchcock did. I tend to show one of Sirk's melodramas—*Imitation of Life, All that Heaven Allows, Magnificent Obsession,* or *Written on the Wind*—about halfway through the course, when the students have begun to understand how films mean and have had some practice searching for and talking about that meaning. On the surface Sirk's films often seem obviously "bad," primarily because they do not conform to Hollywood's dominant codes of realism; their color, for instance, often seems unduly garish, character motivation implausible, and so on. "Heavy-handed," "unbelievable," and "excessive" are adjectives the students invariably use to describe these films. They seem so inferior to the "artsy" films of Eisenstein, Renoir, and others we have screened earlier, inferior even to the Hollywood realism of Ford and Hawks, that the students inevitably assume a superior relationship to Sirk's work. Such an attitude implies a position of some comfort on the part of the students: they have learned something about film analysis, and many become content to rest on that bit of knowledge. But "habit," says Pepper, "simply dulls experience and reduces it to routine" (65). Clearly this is not conducive to that open attitude upon which both aesthetic experience and analytical reasoning are predicated.

In the last decade critics have discovered (and if Sirk hadn't been discovered it would have been necessary for film criticism to invent him) that Sirk was indulging in irony, consciously exaggerating elements of melodrama, a genre popular at the time, so that he could criticize American values and mores and remain commercially viable at the same time. I ask students to be specific, to tell me exactly what is "heavy-handed" or "phony" about *Written on the Wind*. Often they stop here, not resorting to evidence that, in a case such as this, is deceptively difficult and slippery to grasp but appealing instead to "the feeling they got" from the film. They know by this time that this constitutes an insufficient answer, however, and their classmates remind them of this fact. At this point, happily, it is usually not necessary for me to do so. If they do provide a concrete example, it is often the scene in which Dorothy Malone (with the collar of her blouse provocatively up, of course) sits by an obvious studio lake and remembers in voice-over her adolescent romantic daydream involving Rock Hudson. They assume that the lake was meant, as in most Hollywood films, to be taken as real and that the rules of the game require the viewers to suspend their disbelief and pretend that it is real. But this lake looks so artificial that suspension of disbelief is much more difficult, if not impossible. In further discussion I suggest that the phony lake might serve as a metaphor for the false romanticism, the fantasy, of Malone's daydreams (for Hudson had never felt the same way, we find out later) and, moreover, that many of the characters' problems in the film stem from the fact that they rely on surface appearances. When, for example, Robert Stack knocks on Lauren Bacall's door and asks, "Are you decent?" before entering and then discovers that she has gone, we understand what Stack meant by that question, but we can also see that the question has deeper, moral implications that Bacall also understood, which is why she's chosen to leave. Thus, in their experience of the film the class has been trapped into responding to it with the same surface criteria the characters in the film have responded with to each other. They have reacted to the surface of the images instead of examining their implications. This may be an appropriate time to introduce the question of authorial intention, although it isn't necessary; whether Sirk constructed the scene by the lake this way on purpose is, after all, irrelevant to our ability to explicate the work of art.

Both my examples employ a contextualistic approach and, I think, nicely exploit the relationship of the students to film at this point in their aesthetic growth. I believe that this method neither intimidates nor alienates students by introducing them to film through a barrage of facts and terms isolated from their experience. With such an approach as I have outlined here, a conceptual space is established where the teacher and student may meet. For while my responses now are aesthetically more refined, I too at one time breathed a sigh of relief when the roof of Marion's car disappeared under the brackish water and sneered at the artificiality of a Sirkian melodrama. I don't hide this from students; rather, with the benefit of my greater experience in studying film, they see that from once having been in the place they are at now I've gone on to develop my awareness of how films work. My experience, in other words, becomes positive evidence and encouragement for them. Hence, while they may be learning about me, as Fiedler says, they also learn about the material, and, what is just as important, they learn an enthusiasm for it.

It seems to me only logical to introduce students to film in this way, because that is where the meaning of any film begins, with ourselves seated in a theater. Pepper says of subjective experience that "it is ignored, disparaged, or explained away . . . called merely subjective, a result of insufficient analysis, mere vagueness, or nothing but a lot of undiscriminated elements." But, he notes, for the contextualist "it cannot be explained away because it is something in terms of which he explains other things. And for that very reason it cannot be explained. One cannot explain an ultimate fact" (63). Teaching an introduction to film in this way offers the students an opportunity not to attempt the futile task of divorcing themselves from the ultimate fact of their responses but instead to feel comfortable with them and so also with the business of thinking about texts analytically. With this kind of atmosphere in the classroom, where students are encouraged to corroborate and explore their responses to images, the common absence of the primary text is minimized as a problem. The foundation for analytical thinking, equally the goal of the introductory literature class, may in this way successfully be achieved.

Note

*This essay reworks ideas found in my article "Prolegomena to a Contextualist Genre Criticism," *Paunch* nos. 53–54 (Jan. 1980): 138–47; it also appeared in the *Journal of Mind and Behavior* 3.4 (1982): 337–44.

Works Cited

Braudy, Leo. *The World in a Frame*. New York: Anchor, 1977.

Dewey, John. *Art as Experience*. New York: Capricorn, 1958.

Fiedler, Leslie. "Academic Irresponsibility." *Playboy*, Oct.-Dec. 1968, 225, 270–77.

Langer, Suzanne K. "A Note on the Film." In her *Feeling and Form: A Theory of Art*. New York: Scribners, 1953, 211–15.

Metz, Christian. *Film Language: A Semiotics of the Cinema*. Trans. Michael Taylor. New York: Oxford Univ. Press, 1974.

Pepper, Stephen C. *The Basis of Criticism in the Arts*. Cambridge: Harvard Univ. Press, 1965.

A Cinematics Model for Film Studies in Higher Education: Center for Media Study/State University of New York at Buffalo*

Paul Sharits

Dept. responsible for the film program	Center for Media Study
Full-time faculty in the dept.	5
Enrollment policies	
maximum class enrollment (if applicable)	20 (in production courses)
minimum class enrollment	N/A
average class enrollment	30
Staffing	
% of film courses taught by part-time faculty	0%
% taught by full-time instructors or lecturers	0%
% taught by asst., assoc., and full professors	80% (20% by TAs)
Program size	
# of students enrolled in the film program in fall of 1981	600 (30 majors)
# of courses offered in the fall term of 1982	20
# of courses at all levels offered in the program	50
# of students enrolled at the institution	25,000

An important, thoroughly independent, and personal art cinema exists, despite the conspicuous absence of a viable language in which this cinema could be discussed and thereby be more deeply understood. This is not to say that attempts at discussion of the independent cinema have not been made; however, a diagnosis of these attempts most often reveals a deep rupture between the structures of the films and the structures of conventional language modes. This structural rupture is traceable, in part, to typical art school and film school curricula, which tend to reinforce "naturally learned" (unselfcritical) behavioral and cognitive habits.

During my more than eight years of teaching various art-making, art-thinking, and art-historical courses I have noted with distress that most students have enormous difficulty in experiencing, regarding, and discussing their worlds in dynamic terms; these students tend to force rationalistic-static ("everyday," grammatically linear) patterns over dynamic fields ("poems," "paintings,"[1] and so on) and then wonder why they make so little progress in their growth as artists. The problem of having largely static sensibilities becomes acute when the students approach cinema, with its often intricate modulations of temporality, spatiality, and logical or fictive structure. For most students there exist only two basic, crudely divided senses of time—"normal" linear-metric and "psychological" time. Corresponding to this simple Cartesian view, students often have likewise limited conceptions of spatiality and of the potentially multidimensional levels of narrative and non-narrative order relations. What I am calling "cinematics" amounts to an attitude that is both critical of natural and naive conceptions of cinema and insistently open to new definitions of the film-viewing and -making enterprise. This cinematics attitude can generate a comprehensive curriculum that centers on a cinema of exploration and that continually reexamines its premises and objects of research; cinematics naturally supports a milieu wherein change is normative.

My usage of the term cinematics may seem problematical,[2] and its genesis should be explained. In a paper entitled "Words per Page," first presented as an introduction to a course in film production at Antioch College in 1970, I suggested, although I did not fully develop the notion, that the term cinematics replace cinema so that the analytical mode of work and thought I was suggesting to the students would be emphasized. The term was suggested to me by the term linguistics. Because the cinema, as documentation, sociology, entertainment, or art, normatively involves a communicative function, it is not surprising that metaphoric phrases such as "language of film," "grammar of film," and the like are appealing. It should be made clear that while my use of the term cinematics was suggested by the term linguistics, I do not intend to make any isomorphic transpositions. Still, linguistics—because it is not "language" but "the science of language" and because, as a methodology, it offers innumerable morphological, syntactical, and semantic tactics applicable to film composition and comprehension—is a more exacting term than language and grammar. Yet despite the rich analogues connecting cinematics and linguistics, it is wise to make emphatic that cinematics is not subsumed under linguistics. Roman Jakobson, in his notable attempt to locate "poetics" (which deals with the question, "What makes a verbal message a work of art?") integrally within linguistics, points out that a case could be made that linguistics is not an inclusive enough system to deal with poetics: "In short, many poetic features belong not only to the science of language but to the whole theory of signs, that is, to general semiotics. This statement, however, is valid not only for verbal art but also for all varieties of language since language shares many properties with some other systems of signs or even with all of them (pansemiotic features)" (351). If we accept the concept that linguistics is a subset of semiology, it is obvious that a purely linguistic base for cinematics is untenable.

What follows in this paper is, first, a discussion of some of the problems involved in discussing contemporary film art; second, an explanation of the kinds of filmmaking (and videomaking) courses that complement the cinematics model; and third, an overview of various approaches to historical and theoretical courses that can form the armature of a cinematics curriculum. This viewpoint is evolved from personal experiences in filmmaking and film teaching and is not at all intended to be a strict blueprint; it is open for expansion, revision, and clarification.

There is a history of the kind of independent film art considered to be of central importance in this paper. In the 1920s a number of experimental (avant-garde) film works were made, primarily by European painters and sculptors. These works challenged works being made by commercial producers; already, in various degrees and styles, the normative linear time plotting and the illusionary three-dimensional spatiality of the feature film were being seriously complicated. These impressive art films were not widely appreciated, however, and no branch of art criticism or area of university study was developed to accommodate their new articulations of time, motion, and space. Only in Russia, where "formal-minded" filmmaking existed during the 1920s in the feature-length mode, were there developed systematic, theoretic frames of reference that dealt with nontypical film forms (Eisenstein, Pudovkin, Vertov); problematically, montage theories, as interesting and inventive as they were, were interwoven with political conceptions that are less compelling and appropriate today than they were for Russia during the first postrevolutionary decade. A resurgence of art filmmaking occurred in America after World War II, but it was only during the middle 1960s, when a large enough body of significant works existed, that the "new American cinema" was finally recognized as more than an "underground" (seedy, nihilistic) movement. Only the journal *Film Culture* had been consistently critically supportive of the new cinema; no real recognition of the importance of the new work was given by the academic world. Toward the end of the 1960s some private art institutes attempted to integrate experimental film studies into their curricula, but, for the most part, they could not or would not adequately budget these areas, and most such programs have basically failed. In the early 1970s the situation radically changed: established art journals began to publish art film criticism, and a few large universities were developing properly financed art film programs. In spite of this hopeful development, a coherent and sophisticated language about film has not evolved at the same rate as the ever advancing new cinema. Because more and more artist filmmakers are teaching, the problem may resolve itself in time. Nevertheless, there is not much communication between filmmakers regarding their teaching approaches, and it is hard to estimate congruities of approaches, if indeed any exist at all; there appears to be even less interchange between film artists and film critics on this level (consequently, most criticism seems less than inspired).

Forced to dismiss normative, literary, and psychological film theories, just where can one look for models of understanding a cinema that is not primarily narrative or dramatic? A number of filmmakers whose work is under discussion were formerly painters or photographers, and a number of the critics currently interested in their work were critics of abstract art. It is noteworthy that during the 1950s and 1960s a relatively successful vocabulary ("formalism") was employed by critics of painting and sculpture. It was a mode that bypassed the artists' intentions, dismissed "poetic" interpretations, and focused on apt description of the art object; the aim was a certain discreet objectivity. Recently this form of discussing "static" art objects has been used in criticism of independent films; while the intelligence and rigorousness of this approach are laudable, this writing, when applied to film, reads more like a description of a series of connected paintings than like an explication of a unified temporal structure, the film "object." After years of the poetic indulgences of normative film criticism, clever as it often was, it is a pleasure reading the levelheaded descriptive analysis of the formal-oriented critics; however, the built-in assumptions of many of these current analyses, based in nonmoving and nontemporal art-object structural logic, undercut their fine intentions.

Until the middle 1960s, the vocabularies of poetry and music, evolved over centuries to deal with transformation, proved helpful as models for discussions of independent cinema. But with the emergence of analytical, ontological, epistemological, and information-oriented works, these two strategies appear relatively nonapplicable. An argument could be made for the relevance of, say, serial music to film, except that most cinema involves both a musiclike concreteness and nonmusical semantic information (Rosalind Krauss has made a strong case for the sense of non-copresence experienced in perceiving photography and film, and Annette Michelson, borrowing from Peirce's semiology of icon, index, and symbol, convincingly locates photography and film within both indexical and iconic sign levels). Seen in the light of film's semantic information, poetry might appear more closely related to cinema than to music; yet film's referential icon and index character is not necessarily symbolic, if we accept Peirce's distinctions between sign types. Given these problems, how can a curriculum guide students into truly filmic discourses? Before approaching this most difficult question, an important premise and its implications should be explored: the relation theory is to have with practice.

It seems reasonable to suggest that for a student of film to make valuable contributions to the art, either by way of making new works or by critical discourse, the student must grasp both technical and theoretical problems particular to what is being designated here as the art of film. A continual balance of theoretical inquiry and actual filmmaking is integral to a cinematics curriculum, and an undergraduate should not be forced to specialize in either one or the other mode. Following this logic, it is important to suggest a larger curriculum that would support and complement an art-oriented cinema studies area. Art schools that exist totally autonomously from liberal arts colleges probably cannot fulfill these requirements as they most usually have incomplete and/or poor "non-art" curricula. In part, the failure of art schools to support the new art of personal cinema is due to economic difficulties beyond the control of these institutions. What is most distressing is the chronic conservatism of the typical art school; I believe this is due to dependence upon style (rather than upon thought) in "freewheeling" art school contexts. Styles in art naturally change when the thought bases that they manifest shift and grow, but many art schools, because they are often overspecialized and removed from larger social concerns, attempt to sustain curricula in the image of their faculties' own styles. These are the reasons I felt compelled to leave the art school context. In 1970 I began developing Antioch College's film program, which I believed could succeed because the range and variety of "non-art" stimulation afforded students of film art in that context was vast in relation to what could be afforded them in art schools. The program did succeed, in a way that it could not have in an art school. My interest in joining the Center for Media Study at the State University of New York at Buffalo was founded on the premise that SUNY's larger and more diverse resources could even more intensely facilitate students' development of cinematic consciousness. The resources and enthusiasm at SUNY at Buffalo seem capable of developing not only a viable cinema program but a comprehensive temporal media program, including video studies.

Aside from normal liberal arts requirements, I believe it is helpful for the film art student to take courses in psychology (social and perceptual), psychophysiology, semiology, linguistics, mathematics, information sciences, computer programming, art history, poetics, literary studies, theater studies, music theory, studio art, electronics, physics, natural sciences, and, above all, philosophy (particularly those branches of operational philosophy dealing with generalistic and interdisciplinary modes such as general systems).

A media study center would be incomplete without extensive studies in film history (experimental cinema, documentary, classics of the feature film), video history, film criticism (the modes of criticism that have been used, are being used, and could be used in interpreting and evaluating various modes of filmmaking), video criticism, media teaching modes, film analysis (viewing-discussion courses), video analysis, and, of course, film- and video-making courses. All of these general courses can take a multitude of different formats; variation and even contradiction are essential for a dynamic, open, and self-organizing system.

Pursuing the concept of integrated theory and practice, I suggest a further premise: that students simultaneously study both modes with the filmmaker-teacher. The reason for this is opposite to the not-unheard-of tendency of some teachers to indoctrinate students. Ideally, teachers, by splitting their functions into two contexts, can at once be open to and respectful of student-defined forms of enterprise in studio courses as well as being free, in the theory context, to elucidate their own and others' thoughts on what constitutes an aesthetics of film. Teachers further students' growth by having empathy with students' unique motives (helping students discover these motives), and by presenting new thoughts to students, teachers clarify and/or challenge the students' own conceptions. Teachers need not suppress their unique formulations in order to guide students toward self-realization. Seen in this light, it is obvious that to force "theory" into "practice" situations would be to distract students from organic creative growth. Cinematics cannot be simply a system of perceiving and regarding cinema but should be likened to a multidimensional field of inquisitiveness, wherein relativistic, probabilistic attitudes coexist with more axiomatic views. Flexibility and humor facilitate serious engagement. Certainly some basic principles, shared by all those engaged in a research mode, would also seem necessary—yet the search for such principles is much of the substance of research itself and so definitive principles are difficult to form (perhaps it is this that lends the task its richness and seductiveness). Many different modes of method, thought, and form can be integrally subsumed in a general cinematics process-frame (e.g., the often stated differentiations between "narrative" and "non-narrative" are not to be regarded as conclusive—so many ironic and straightforward convolutions of these "disparate polarities" have been woven into convincing films that to think of them as distinct categories is now impossible). The most basic principle of cinematics, its vortex, is that student and teacher share the analytic research attitude; exploratory, experimental behavior is of higher value than any specific methodological stance or any specific designation of acceptable content. Still, works and theories exhibiting experimental-analytical concerns form the most compelling research area. (Note that "research," in this context, refers both to "study" and to "creative work.") What might distinguish this approach from scientific approaches is that no solution to the issues raised is necessarily postulated; attitude and behavior—"process"—are more important than conclusiveness.

There are probably innumerable ways in which a research frame of reference can manifest itself in film- and video-making courses. But there exists one approach that is as damaging to creative development as it is common to normative film-making courses: this is the approach that overstresses technical "professionalism," assuming the innate correctness of whatever (arbitrary) school of thought it follows. The appeal of this approach is evident: it easily gratifies the students' desires for absolutes and it relieves the instructors from confrontation with the individual student's actual needs as a unique creator. It is interesting that most of the film artists who are presently teaching filmmaking courses never had "formal" technical training in film. I would suggest that no program be based on traditional (i.e., ultimately commercial) technical production models. The program that avoids destruction of individuality while providing the student with basic skills is no casual matter; this problem forms the core of my suggestions for a curriculum.

While traditional professional techniques and procedures should not be the core of introductory filmmaking courses, some of these techniques are valuable for the students to know from the beginning. These techniques should presumably be presented in logical and pragmatic progression but should not be permeated with an air of being "fundamental"; these techniques should be regarded both as simply operational and as having some organic relation to the unique motives that arise for the student as a whole human being and artist. This apparently paradoxical proposition does not disclose a hopelessly impossible conception. The Bauhaus, with at least some small success, faced such a task, and something from the Bauhaus concern with "the whole man" must be applicable to our problem. The easiest solution may be found in having the student begin his or her studies in a protocinema framework so that the subsequent technical developments of cinema proper would naturally suggest themselves, before being presented in the introductory filmmaking course.

Another sort of course that might be of value is one in which the most broad investigation of the documentary-recording functions of cinema would be undertaken, without any particular stylistic goals being stressed. Instead of stressing the typical social and/or anthropological approach, one would attend to film's pure indexical structures (light types, lenses, emulsions) and procedures (microcinematography, photospectrometry, time-lapse, thermography, "Kirlian" or radiation field cinematography, etc.). The use of fluorescent, ultraviolet, polarized, infrared, laser, X-ray, and other radiation systems would be experimentally studied in their image-forming relations with variously sensitized film stocks. The iconic and symbolic limits and implications of recording and projecting should be the ongoing center of discussion in such a course; the large danger that such a course could become purely technical and sterile would have to be continually, consciously checked. Technical, perceptual, and conceptual dimensions should be reflected back and forth among each other at each level of study. In recent years a great deal of the most interesting art has in some way or another connected with scientific and/or philosophic investigations, in either subjects or techniques. There is no reason why this tendency could not find a secure place in a cinematics curriculum.

Video-making courses would be pursued in a manner that would explore imagery and techniques that are implicit in the structure and function of video as a perceptual and physical system. Students might even be required to work with both film and video; these media obviously share characteristics, but it is important that students study their many differences. One way the crucial differences of these media could become explicit is by developing a course in which the student would transpose imagery back and forth between the media, attempting a balanced hybridic synthesis while also noticing and emphasizing the transformation of the imagery that would occur at each stage of such an interplay.

At intermediate and advanced levels of film study and filmmaking more and more complex recording systems should be presented and explored for their imagistic potentials, while, simultaneously, the student should also be encouraged to follow deep personal inclinations. A flexible curriculum will also respect the value of some more structured courses: if the artist-teacher is personally intent on deeply exploring a particular system it is obvious that, properly presented, the course of this investigation could be profitably followed by students—probably the students' work could also be of aid to the artist-teacher. The artist who teaches knows full well how much these two roles often overlap and at times become indistinguishable. It is possible that this can cause confusion and distress to everyone concerned—the teacher, the students, the administrators of the program. It is also possible that a wonderful symbiosis among all these elements of the general system can occur, benefiting each member of the relationship and, from this, effecting a continual betterment of the system itself. Most institutions recognize this in at least one sense: faculty members, whose technically defined role is "to teach," are also encouraged, by various "faculty development awards," to go on learning and growing in their special areas. Institutions with graduate programs also appoint graduate students to teachers as research and teaching assistants. This often does not work well in art departments because of displaced notions of "individualism"; this is hard to define precisely but I believe most art educators have encountered and understand this selfish form of individualism (which makes potentially valuable group projects in studio classes so hard to guide). The individualism, a form of subjectivism that is usually dignified by recourse to romantic interpretations of art historical figures, is not the kind of student self-development and self-realization that can exist in a research-oriented, democratically structured cinematics curriculum, where sharing is essential and a mood of friendliness is most pragmatic.

An open, symbiotic system can be modeled by extending and developing the teacher's special interests into graduate-level courses wherein the students can peer directly into their teacher's art-making processes and expand their own abilities by participating in the creation of the teacher-artist's projects. It is assumed that the teacher's special interests and style of working are more advanced than the students' and that the teacher is a worthwhile enough artist that he or she has something creational to impart to the student in such a learning-by-doing situation. My own work is exploratory and expanding, not an attempt to polish more and more carefully a particular style. During the past three years I have found that when several of my best students work with me on my projects—salaried and doing twenty to thirty hours of work a week—I am able to teach more of what I know of my art than I can in normative classroom situations. In working with me, the student assistant is called on to be technically inventive and to participate in creative formulation of the project, not just to do tedious dirty work. The student learns, in an adventurous and professional context, advanced techniques and, more abstractly, learns my modes of problem solving, scheduling, organizing complex projects, and inventing alternative financial strategies, things that are impossible to impart effectively in the typical studio classroom, where I am attempting to focus my attention on the students' not so complex self-defined projects. The assistant can selectively draw upon this more practical knowledge in structuring his or her own life and work as an artist. Group work is not an innovative conception of student-teacher relationships; it has been a general practice in many research-oriented university departments and has been used where group study is normative (i.e., dance and theater). Nevertheless, group work has specific problems and probably cannot be jumped into without some degree of gradual adjustment for both the teacher and the student.

When film art education is posed in these terms, one can begin to envision the transactional relation of teacher and students as a research team; this is in opposition to hierarchical-patriarchal interactional teaching systems that nondemocratically mask the teacher as intrinsically superior to the student. Observed this way, cinematics has its axiology.

The range of theoretical and historical courses that complement the kind of filmmaking courses I've suggested remains to be discussed. Where does the student begin to grasp the state of his or her art? How does he or she progress toward more and more deep and subtle understandings?

The central concern of the curriculum I am proposing is with the avant-garde film but this does not preclude interest in the history and theory of the normative documentary cinema and the commercial feature-length cinema. Certainly there are overlapping concerns and techniques, and these should be studied. As I already stated, the student should have as comprehensive an understanding as possible of the totality of human temporal ordering; traditional values and concepts should be explored, if only to critique and dismiss them as too insufficient for operational usage. It would seem that a film criticism course would adequately explore such traditional conceptions (i.e., the theories of Bazin, Kracauer, et al.). Historical studies would concurrently round out such critiques. In these areas perhaps a semiological approach is reasonable, but it seems unlikely that the semiological study of narrativity has much bearing on works that do not conceal their deep structures within a fictive order. Responding to and understanding nonfictive, often self-analytical works (which are the primary consideration of cinematics) present different sets of problems.

It is usual that a discipline is introduced to students from a historical point of view; however, there is no way of ensuring that the understanding of any one film will occur by following chronological development of styles—in fact it is likely that this approach, used exclusively, will reinforce the "natural attitude" (atomistic categorization as a way of "knowing") and mislead the student. Historical knowledge of any area is indispensable to the serious student of that area; but if one of the primary aims of education in film is to enable the student to develop a sense of transformational structures, then a purely rationalist, static, linear view of film will obviously obfuscate that intention. The diachronic view could be of use if it framed itself within a specifically focused thematic context (e.g., following the threads of the seminal American "psychodramatic" film form through later subjectivist manifestations to the eventual reversal of the film viewer's role, from being an observer of a protagonist's inner world to direct self-reflection during the act of observing). But the whole logic of studying art from thematic reference frames, grouping works by style characteristics—by far the most prevalent "appreciation course" technique—could stand some scrutiny; certainly, if the student is offered this approach exclusively and from one point of view, it will be crippling to the student's individualistic growth. The student may be able to group together sets of works, which has some value, but may still not have gained a capacity to experience deeply any one work. This ability to group works together, even when done with wit and finesse, may not be of central use to the student who desires to make films. It should go without saying that both chronological and thematic survey modes are valuable; what I am stressing is that these approaches have limitations and if they are employed exclusively one can make strong predictions that the students' education will be incomplete, perhaps in fundamental ways.

What follows suggests the forms a cinematics approach might take in the aesthetic-studies dimension and describes a basic three-level division of types of study, in a progressive order: interpretive cinematics, analytical cinematics, and speculative cinematics. There is not just one mode of interpretation or of analysis or of speculation, so it is obvious that I am not speaking of simply three courses with fixed form and content. On the contrary, each of these three general approaches will take any number of varying emphases.

Interpretive courses are those that present and discuss works in historical and/or thematic modes. While specific analytical methodologies can be mentioned, it is not the task of these courses to deeply analyze individual works. Here the student is introduced to the longitudes and the latitudes of the cinema that has been called experimental, poetic, underground, non-narrative, psychodramatic, personal. The task is to give the student an overview of the art-film movement, to interpret its general tendencies, to become aware of its most important artists and of their stated aesthetic intentions. At higher course levels, interpretive courses might intensively study a particular historical period and the relationships the films might have to other concurrent art forms, or intensive study of a particular style (say, surrealism and automatism) could be pursued, or in-depth studies could be made of single artists who have created a significant body of work and who have had measurable influence on the development of film art.

What distinguishes analytical courses from what I am calling interpretive courses is that the films that are viewed analytically need not have any historical or stylistic connection. In fact, the works shown should be highly differentiated so that what is consistent is the testing of specific analytical modes; the search is for discovering or developing a general language, capable of application to any number of film works. The individual film—largely divorced from the contexts of its maker's intentions and its stylistic or historical relations to other films—is what is being directly attended to. Such analysis could proceed along, say, structuralist or phenomenological lines. A structuralist approach would investigate the layers of consciousness that different works elicit in viewers. I personally feel that phenomenological research should be clearly distinguished from the sort of psychoanalytical interpretation of "meaning" of content that is so typical in literature courses and in courses dealing with narrative cinema. Naturally, some surrealist and psychodramatic works can be interpreted as dreamlike, but I would suggest that these films do not constitute the most appropriate kind of work for phenomenological analysis, because while they picture the dream state and invite viewers to participate in dream logic, they do not induce a dream state in an individual viewer. Some "minimal" films, which do not guide the viewer along a narrative or a directive formal development, provide viewers with an open field within which the individual viewer can enter dreamlike states of consciousness; these synchronic films may be most appropriate to phenomenological analysis. Films that are themselves dreams or dreamlike are perhaps better analyzed with structuralist tools.

In introducing speculative cinematics, some points should be made concerning the role of humor in creative work. Perhaps the tone of objectivity that runs through this paper will lead the reader to assume that it presents too severe a model for an art curriculum. In fact, just as there exists a great deal more humor in so-called minimal or structural cinema than most viewers at first recognize, there is more lightness in my views than might immediately be inferred. These views are predicated on the belief that self-development, which does depend on the opening and releasing of the "subjective self," does not necessarily involve neurotically morbid excesses or autistic self-indulgence but that the individual's inner world coincides positively with external reality and social life (the "objective" dimensions). Integral to humor is playfulness. ("To keep your art young you have to imitate animals. What do they do? They play." Constantin Brancusi.) To speculate is to play. Speculation is a natural activity in a relativistic, probabilistic world. At a certain point, where one might measure, if one could, a 180-degree shift in the angle of sensibility, one hopes that the student recognizes the humor inevitably attached to a pursuit of an essentialistic cinema. This humor may or may not be a laughing matter, but it certainly can be used to generate a speculative subject matter. The problem that presents itself is: how does one tell what is humorous, in distinction to what is serious but idiotic, or what is absurd but "feels" utterly pedestrian, or what is substructurally humorous but masks itself in an attempt to remove itself from the level of joking, or what is joking without being funny? Fortunately, one is not called upon, in speculating, to be sternly comic; the alternative to rigid humor is not crystalline seriousness but an outlook aimed at what lies beyond both humor and seriousness—the unthought, the undone, the unfelt.

The most important consideration in determining the nature of what such hypothetical thinking should be is, finally, its functional outcome for the student, what will facilitate a student's growth when he or she is beyond the security of studenthood. By graduate school, the student has gained another form of security: a grasp of his or her subject. This means that the student can not only withstand a bit of irony, and appreciate it, but also may need it to loosen up what may have become for that student a premature calcification of attitude and style. Humor and seriousness may coexist in a single pursuit or object or thought; an idea that at first appears humorous may upon deeper reflection reveal itself as being very serious—this is the kind of irony that could be employed in construing areas for speculation. The speculation cannot be mere fantasy, innocuous toying about. It should involve the posing of difficult questions, perhaps questions that are ultimately unanswerable but that can serve to direct the mind into realism beyond logic. Many important artists have set goals beyond what can be possibly achieved and have left for us marvelous, if not absolutely successful, tracings of their reaching ever beyond themselves (one thinks of Cézanne, in his old age, complaining endlessly that he just could not get "it" right).

Anyone who would venture to "teach" a speculative course would have to have, personally, some self-challenging, unanswered (perhaps unanswerable) art questions and a willingness to share these questions with students. Curiosity about something is not strong enough to guide such a course; there must be an intensity in the wondering process to sustain it through its inevitable "dead-end" frustrations. I am interested in this kind of course because there are some questions, at the heart of my own filmmaking, that at once elude me and guide me on.

In summation, what is being argued for in this paper is an educational milieu that allows for and encourages a synthesis of rigorous thought and independent inventiveness—a seriousness free of dogmatism. The "optimal student" is one who will graduate in possession of necessary technical and theoretical skills without being bound by them, who will utilize these skills as tools and not as ends in themselves. This intelligent and imaginative student has as much confidence in his or her sense of self as in the contents of his or her education.

Notes

*This is an edited version of a paper that appeared in both the *Quarterly Review of Film Studies* 1 (1976): 394–416, and *Film Culture*, nos. 65–66 (1978): 43–68.

[1] In my view, paintings and other creations that involve temporality in their making and in our experiencing of them should be regarded as dynamic rather than static, even though these objects are not physically kinetic.

[2] It should be pointed out that there exist strong criticisms of this usage. Hollis Frampton and Annette Michelson make convincing arguments for the use of "film" over "cinema" when discussing certain modes of independent filmmaking (Frampton, "For a Metahistory of Film," *Artforum*, Sept. 1971; Michelson, "Paul Sharits and the Critique of Illusionism," *Projected Images*, Walker Art Center, 1974). "Cinematics," because it is derived from "cinema," which refers more to film's illusions of movement than it does to the immanent tangibilities of the film object, may not reflect well enough the ontological and/or epistemological orientations of the filmmaking that I wish to portray. Yet I have not found a term that comfortably replaces cinematics; words such as filmatics seem somewhat clumsy. Also, my approach does not strictly deny the reality—in consciousness—of film's illusions of motion and spatiality.

Works Cited

Jakobson, Roman. "Linguistics and Poetics." In *Style in Language*. Ed. Thomas A. Sebeok. Cambridge: MIT Press, 1966, 351.

Krauss, Rosalind. "Problems of Criticism, X: Pictorial Space and the Question of Documentary." *Artforum*, Nov. 1971, 68–71.

Michelson, Annette. "Art and the Structuralist Perspective." In *The Future of Art*. New York: Viking, 1970, 37–59.

Sharits, Paul. "Words per Page." *Afterimage*, no. 4 (Autumn 1972), 26–42.

An Open Approach to Film Study and the Situation at Iowa

Dudley Andrew

Dept. responsible for the film program   Department of Communication and
  Theater Arts, Division of Broadcasting and Film
Full-time faculty in the dept.   5 (film department)
                                             9 (Division of Broadcasting and Film)
Enrollment policies
  maximum class enrollment (if applicable)   N/A
  minimum class enrollment   N/A
  average class enrollment   33
Staffing
  % of film courses taught by part-time faculty   0%
  % taught by full-time instructors or lecturers   40% (TAs)
  % taught by asst., assoc., and full professors   60%
Program size
  # of students enrolled in the film program in fall of 1981   60 undergraduates
  # of undergraduate courses offered in the fall term of 1981   13
  # of courses at all levels offered in the program   26
  # of students enrolled at the institution   27,400

When the organization of film study is discussed on our campuses, we are essentially discussing power and possession. None of us can claim to be aloof from these impulses, because our interest in the subject comes from wanting to borrow, acquire, or use the strength of films, whether we are teaching a film or trying to lobby for a film budget. If we go out of our way in the interest of film, we have entered the great stock market of educational capitalism. It is important that we become aware of our own honest interests and the way those interests conflict with the interests of others (fellow teachers, administrators, and students) who would also, in some way or other and to various extents, like to possess film.

The administrative struggle for the allocation of institutional resources of money, staff, and degrees depends on the results of the power struggle among shareholders, who debate pedagogy and vie for control of the study of film and ultimately of those resources. The history of this debate is instructive and recapitulates many of the great issues in humanistic education over the last half century. Film study was born as an adjunct to the study of other disciplines when it was discovered that film swelled enrollments in English, theater, art, and journalism and that it accorded a certain prestige to those teachers who knew how to harness its energy. In this paradigm, still active today, film is treated as a recent instance of a traditional source of values (mythic, aesthetic, sociological), and it is seen as the instance most capable in our era of relaying the innate power of that source to a large audience.

Film societies in the late fifties grew up to the side of these other disciplines in part to dispute this claim. Each week film societies proclaimed that film was valuable in itself and not because it camouflaged some older values traditionally studied in universities. For many students and faculty these screenings set the emotional tone for the week and cued coffeehouse and classroom discussion in an informal manner.

Naturally, it wasn't long before academics came along to capitalize on all this loose energy and began establishing film programs, majors, divisions, and departments. By and large they rested their claim on a knowledge of film history and a feeling for the importance of certain auteurs. In other words, they achieved sovereignty by reason of a privileged set of films that defined the field and that they claimed knowledge of and a right to. Anyone teaching films outside that set clearly was teaching something other than film and anyone using correct films but outside the program was doubtless misusing them (that is, teaching values irrelevant to film qua film).

This state couldn't last. Academic film tycoons who set the market value of every film by buying up auteurs cheaply (only to sell them later at great profit) were attacked because the nature of their work seemed improper in a university. They are essentially collectors and buffs, whose work is closer to connoisseurship than to scientific research.

The group planning the overthrow of the academic film tycoons may be called the analysts. They offered methods by which to study any given film rather than a list of films to be studied. They realized that power in the university comes not from possessing objects of worth (rocks, flowers, films) but by way of a particular technique that transforms those objects into a certain kind of knowledge called geology, botany, or film analysis.

The technique that resulted from the effort of the analysts consists of factoring out from any film specifically cinematic values and processes. The expert commands power by an ability to recognize such values and rewards those students who differentiate films on the basis of the largest number of differing traits (editing, angle, music, etc.) or who can pinpoint the key trait in a given film (the tracking shot in a film by Max Ophuls). The teacher-analyst also wields power by deciding which films are likely to best illustrate the workings of "the cinematic." Indeed, a history of the cinema can be created by the expert as well as by the connoisseur, though it most probably would consist of a series of clips from films exemplifying the developing potential of the medium.

Structuralism, semiotics, and poststructuralism are the furthest developments of this tendency. In one sense, these movements amount to a counterrevolution, power having been lifted from those who professed a narrow technique (film analysis) and given to those whose techniques are valorized by the prestige they have in other disciplines (linguistics, Marxism, psychoanalysis).

In surveying this great cycle of the development of film study we can see one constant. In each era and among each group there exists a privileged list (be it films, traits, methods) whose possession guarantees the group supremacy and for whose possession each group would readily ossify film study. The results of this parochialism have been film buffism among the auteurists and obscurantism among the analysts. In both cases, special knowledge protects the empowered class. And this is disappointing because we all thought at one time that film study could serve as the focus for a renovation of the liberal arts. Instead it has fallen prey to the specialization and professionalization that have made academic departments bastions of entrenched power and tradition rather than fields of inquiry.

I would like to point out that this kind of power struggle has been fought innumerable times before. In the Middle Ages the Bible was at the center of such a debate. When a class of hermeneutes was given authority over the interpretation of that text it meant uniformity and political power. A strict rule-bound game (consisting of interpretation at the four levels of literal, symbolic, analogic, and anagogic meaning) suppressed all other games. The Church protected this uniformity by condemning all personal uses of the book as heretical and deserving of excommunication.

Today we have university provosts and deans conferring on groups of experts the right of interpretation in film. While expertise certainly brings with it a measure of authority, I fear the repressive authority that departments have always claimed in order to protect the interests of that expertise.

While there is nothing that compels a film department or its members to adopt closed attitudes, I suspect this is the way of the academic world. After all, these same attitudes are exemplified in their own manner by all traditional disciplines. In struggling for autonomy and departmental status, film teachers are likely to take on these attitudes as means or ends, establishing a list of films that harbor obvious or astutely embedded cinematic treasures and insisting on the use of a special vocabulary for the study of these films. In this way they protect themselves in the name of "the field" or "professional film scholarship."

This overall system leads to rewarding students who do not think beyond, or change, the rules of the game. It encourages players to be hostile to those talking about film in other ways. It demands, in other words, a certain initiation into the game. It is my belief that this attitude is fostered and protected by the autonomous film program that formalizes rules and that thrives largely because of its guardianship of those rules. It has been authorized to develop "standards" and to rebuke any discussion of film that takes place outside those standards, that is, that takes place elsewhere and by other rules.

Clearly it would be inhuman to suggest that film discussion should occur without standards and without the constant inspection of those standards. What is surprising and troublesome, however, is the desire students, faculty, and administrators have to codify those standards so soon and so thoroughly; to say that film study ought to go on in this building and that if it goes on in another it must do so without credit.

No doubt I show a certain cynicism or at least a pessimism in this discussion of the departmental structure of our undergraduate educational process. Departments, it seems to me, are political and economic companies determined to grow to the largest possible size by using all normal means of advertising, competition, and self-interest. They demand production from their senior members in terms of publications and blind adherence from their graduate students. Recently they have begun insisting that majors remain more and more within the department to hold enrollments up. This has been facilitated by the diminution of liberal arts core and breadth requirements and the implicit encouragement at all levels of strong undergraduate specialization.

To reward the field of film by conferring on it departmental status ironically saps from it a native strength it possesses that otherwise could help implement radical changes in liberal education.

I believe the greatest eras of film study have already passed us by. When Louis Delluc presided over the film club movement in Paris in the early twenties, scholars and aficionados from all the arts gathered together and, on the basis of a naive interest in film, generated the excitement we call the impressionist movement. What went on then in terms of film discussion, film journals, and actual filmmaking was to me education at its most real and important level. Then again in Paris, right after World War II, André Bazin led a revival of this film club atmosphere, a revival of film journals, and a revival of independent filmmaking, all outside the university. Bazin was, in my estimation, the greatest film educator we have yet had, although he was barred from the university. Anything we can preserve of the natural interdisciplinary approach to film exemplified by these eras is worth the insecurity and chaos we may feel by operating in a nondepartmental manner.

Of course we don't live in such a vibrant, fluid, or general milieu as those in Paris did following both great wars. Students are looking for easy majors, professors for easy courses or ones to make them popular. The nondepartmental system, it must be admitted, permits a degree of charlatanism that would appall those seriously interested in the development of both students and the field. Let me suggest, however, that on large campuses, at least, the natural economy of the educational process will eventually eradicate gross misuse of the medium. Those professors who teach film seriously and creatively will outlive those sycophants who cling pathetically to the field. Administrators and students will force the latter to return to their home areas and will encourage the former to more daring discoveries in film. Indeed, it has been my experience that many of the greatest sycophants sit solidly in departments of film from which they cannot be removed. They profess no other discipline and, no matter how ineptly, they nonetheless teach film with the imprimatur of the film department. In the nondepartmental model, film teachers must convince their students, their peers, and their deans that they can profitably add to liberal education by offering a film course. The situation,

I confess, might readily be different at the small college, where the coefficient of competition is decisively lower.

But for campuses of all sizes I think the film center model is a substantial improvement over the film department model. Let me sketch some aspects of a film center. Depending on interest and funding there would be:

1. A clearinghouse of information concerning film courses being offered throughout the university, presided over by an adviser or advisers who would try to orchestrate the scheduling of these courses and who would advertise them. Clearly such an adviser would need to be well schooled in the medium and realize the impact on film of literature, psychology, linguistics, art history, etc.

2. A facility for film study equipped with projectors, viewers, purchased prints, frame enlargers, a film rental desk, and classrooms. If available, filmmaking equipment would be maintained at the center.

3. Courses in the theory and techniques of filmmaking and film analysis taught by the adviser(s) and their graduate students at the center. Presumably, most graduate students would be involved in an intensive two-year program (M.A.) or, in rare cases, would serve as long-term (four-year) research apprentices working with the center's advisers. Graduate education is another question entirely, but it would surely draw heavily on graduate seminars in related areas while it focused on film through seminars and individual projects at the center itself.

4. The film major. Obviously, I am not in favor of a vast and delineated major. The film center is designed to allow and encourage the interaction of professors and majors from various fields over a subject of common interest—film. But film could act as an appropriate major for some undergraduates who might use it to acquire the disciplines and investigate the problems that have always been at the heart of the ideology of liberal arts education. As Ortega once said, education's major goal in our century is to teach the need for education. Insofar as film encourages students to learn linguistics, French, psychology, and art history and does not multiply courses on genres and auteurs, it could serve this goal perhaps better than any other major in the university.

Guidelines for minimum and maximum amounts of film courses, requisite outside study, specification of film areas to be covered (production, history, analysis, sociology, etc.) could all be worked out without the film adviser's dictating the precise content of the major. At the University of Iowa, which has a traditional film division, we have tried to create the impact of a center by reducing departmental requirements, encouraging and cross-listing appropriate film offerings from other departments, and demanding that our majors branch out into other departments.

It seems to me that this kind of attitude is the only justification for a film major. Admittedly, all this does not completely rid us of the specter of the expert (for what else are advisers and graduate students?), but it does acknowledge film to be a trigger for discovery and not a product to be consumed. At its best, film spurs students to confront other disciplines, other students, other methods, other arts, and even other films than the ones currently hypostatized in the film departments some of us are struggling to create or protect.

To me, films are both cultural objects to be mastered and experiences that continually master us. Film buffs are mere collectors of experiences (their own or those of the auteurs they worship), and film scientists protect themselves from experience by a certain technique of mastery. Education, I believe, is best served by a dialectic that forces us to interrogate films and then to interrogate ourselves in front of films. We must learn to experience, to remove ourselves from experience, to understand experience, and then to reexperience in what amounts to a perpetual internal revolution. The temptation to halt this flight of education, a temptation that is at once psychological and political, is the desire to fixate, possess, and fetishize some aspects of a process whose value derives precisely from this flight. Film departments block out the field and position the "I" before it. Every true film education, in search of the field and in search of the "I," must strive to overturn the security of this situation.

The University of Iowa is committed to retaining the liberal arts emphasis within the study of communications systems. A mixture of production and scholarly work attends every degree program. We have definitively rejected the M.F.A. degree in order to eliminate any "all production" emphasis. M.A. candidates must be able to do scholarly work and to write extended papers and exams. On the other hand, no undergraduate or master's candidate may graduate without having produced films or video, and all must have a more than rudimentary knowledge of production techniques. While production does not figure in the Ph.D. degree in any formal way, all candidates are urged to acquire skill in this area. Only a very few doctoral students in the last decade have left Iowa without significant mastery in production of film and/or video.

This emphasis on the liberal arts basis of our discipline also leads to an open major and master's program. We do not encourage the amassing of credits in the division and we make considerable use of other departments. An undergraduate major may receive a degree with just twenty-four credit hours of work in film and video, though most take more. Through our close relations to these other departments, we emphasize work in foreign language, in philosophy and literature, in psychology and sociology, in music, art, and art history. Iowa's renowned writers' workshop sends us both teachers and students.

Some attempt is made to provide an overall "communications" and "arts" context for the study of film/video. This is readily accomplished by drawing on aspects of our parent department, communication and theater arts. Playwrights and actors from drama work in our productions. Rhetorical studies and mass communications courses deal strongly with film.

Currently we are responding to the general "professional" emphasis shift in the liberal arts, trying to attract students from business and journalism with varied programs in corporate communication, visual culture, and so forth. This complicates the self-image we have constructed over the years as a nonprofessional division where talented students can learn the skills needed for a profession if they so choose. In addition, we are trying to blend film and broadcasting in our production sequence, for in fact our division is split between broadcasting and film. A separate head coordinates the work of each half. A single faculty member heads the whole production area. Generally we work by means of local expertise, each faculty member making decisions over a small portion of the program but checking with the departmental chairman. There is no formal student committee or lobby, though representatives are selected and can, on an irregular basis, make student opinions and demands formally felt.

The informal and flexible nature of the program's administration extends to individual student programs as well, where advising takes precedence over rules and where student-initiated ideas are frequently actualized. A clear example of this lies in our refusal to encourage a mini-Hollywood atmosphere in our production courses. Students are responsible for organizing their productions as they see fit. There is no official "crew" system one must work through. This, we have found, promotes a healthy diversity in film styles and in working methods.

We feel that we are able to offer such freedom because of two important factors, the trust of the university in our academic integrity and the working conditions we enjoy with other departments. Iowa's film program is one of the oldest, if not the oldest, in the country, courses being on record from the World War I era and a curriculum dealing with film existing since World War II. It has always been lodged in the Department of Communication and Theater Arts, generally regarded as the top department of its kind in the country. This has given the program in film plenty of internal respect. Its quality and mission have never been questioned by the administration.

Our rapport with other departments is, I believe, the most valuable asset we possess. Cross-listing of courses is routine. Team teaching is frequent. The head of the film division holds a joint appointment with the program in comparative literature. There is a formal Ph.D. subprogram entitled "Film-French" with a standing committee composed of members of our program and the French department. We have been and expect to be a program that attracts students from around the university. Given our rapport with other departments, we find students from every major infiltrating our courses and broadening their scope in the process. Those students who elect to be majors in film profit from this exposure to music, art, writing, philosophy, and psychology students, since all of them have come in search of something that fascinates them, the cinema. It is our task to promote, extend, and reflect upon this fascination.

Requirements for a B.A. with Emphasis in Broadcasting and Film

A minimum of twenty-four semester hours in the Department of Communication and Theater Arts is required for majoring in broadcasting and film. The program is intended for the student who seeks an understanding of the nature of the broadcast and film media and their relationship to the larger field of the communication arts. The program is offered within the context of a liberal education and is not regarded solely as preparation for a professional career. Students may emphasize either broadcasting or film in their selection of elective courses, but minimal requirements will lead all students to exposure to historical and evaluative courses in both broadcasting and film and experience in the production of materials of broadcast and film media.

Requirements for a major in the Division of Broadcasting and Film are:

1. Division course required of all majors: 36B:035 Introduction to Broadcasting and Film Production.
2. Minimum of six semester hours of advanced (100-level or above) production in the Division of Broadcasting and Film.
3. Minimum of nine semester hours of nonproduction courses in the Division of

Broadcasting and Film, at least six of which must be 100-level courses or above.

4. Minimum of two courses from either the Division of Dramatic Art or from the Division of Rhetorical Studies.

Courses (only film-related courses are listed)

36B:25: Mass Media and Mass Society   Introduction to the history and theory of the mass media of communication, with emphasis on radio, television, and the motion picture.

36B:35: Introduction to Broadcasting and Film Production   For the student with no previous experience; the course is project-oriented, with a short video production, short Super-8 films, and audio production required; emphasis on formative principles and effectiveness of communication.

36B:35: Introduction to Film Analysis   Methods of analyzing various kinds of films, with emphasis on "classic" narrative works from the American and European traditions; methods studied include shot-by-shot breakdown, narrative segmentation, auteur, and genre.

36B:51: Survey of Film   Introduction to motion-picture history, theory, and criticism, including study of relationship of film to other arts, film screenings included.

36B:52: Film and Society   The role of the motion picture in contemporary society; consideration of issue of censorship and treatment of social issues.

36B:114: Film Production I   Advanced Super-8 production course devoted to film structure and technique; cameras, editing equipment, and necessary stock provided for the four films students make in experimenting with various modes and genres. Prerequisites: 36B:35 and consent of instructor.

36B:115: Film Production II   Advanced production practices in 16mm, sync-ground editing, camera and recording techniques; class discussion of student work; emphasis on technical and aesthetic aspects. Prerequisites: 36B:114 and consent of instructor.

36B:116: Film Workshop   Independent creative work for students who have shown outstanding talent in 36B:115. A budget and facilities are provided for the completion of a proposed film. Prerequisite: consent of instructor.

36B:117: Special Topics in Film Production   For advanced students. Subjects such as animation, industrial organization, editing, and special effects are elaborated by local and visiting professional filmmakers.

36B:119: Practicum in Broadcasting and Film   Internship experience working in professional media organizations. Available on pass/fail basis only. Prerequisite: consent of instructor.

36B:121: New Directions in Video   For advanced television and art students interested in pursuing the artistic potential of video; conceptual, performance, and graphic approaches explored.

36B:126: Technology of Film Production   Technical bases (optics, chemistry, film stocks, camera design, sound recording, editing, and lab practices) of film production.

36B:128: Broadcasting and Film Writing   Exercises in visualization, sequencing, and dialogue; preparation of treatment and screenplay for a theatrical or television fiction film; tutorial and small group discussions of script problems.

May be repeated. Prerequisites: courses in broadcasting and film study or production, and advanced work in writing.

36B:134: Film and Public Policy   Preparation of proposals for public policy based on historical research into problems of official and unofficial censorship, government investigations of violence and obscenity, government sponsorship and production of films, and subsidy for television, film, and other arts.

36B:136: Documentary and Public Issues Broadcasting   Forms and functions of documentary in print, photography, radio, motion pictures, and television; emphasis on historical development of the television documentary and its use in sociopolitical persuasion in our society; screening of programs from important television series.

36B:141: Documentary Film   Historical and critical survey of the documentary as reportorial, experiential, and persuasive form; screenings emphasize work of Flaherty, Grierson, Lorentz, and recent cinema verité directors.

36B:142: Film and Ideology   Study of films and theories illuminating relationships between producers of images, consumers of images, and structure of images; often focuses on particular types of films, for example, those about women or violence or politics.

36B:145: The American Film   Interrelations of industry, genres, and directors that make up the "Hollywood complex."

36B:146: European Film History   Movements in Europe most significant in film history; silent cinemas of Sweden, Germany, and Russia; films of France in the 1930s; postwar Italian cinema.

36B:147: French Cinema   History of film in French culture; lectures on French culture, analysis of films, and discussion of relation of filmmakers to politics, religion, etc.

36B:148: National Cinema   The history of the cinema and its relation to the culture of England, Italy, Japan, Germany, or Russia.

36B:149: Film Criticism   Study of the purposes, presuppositions, and styles of film criticism; major theoretical positions related to various areas of concern to film critics; theoretical dimensions reflected in writings of the students.

36B:150: Film Theory   Introduction to major theoretical positions: Gombrich and Arnheim v. Kracauer; Eisenstein and Pudovkin v. Bazin; structuralism v. phenomenology; recent developments in theory introduced.

36B:152: The Sexes and Film   Surveys American films from 1920s to 1970s, centering on questions, what are the images of the sexes in the films viewed? and how do these images relate to society?

36B:155: Literature and the Film

36B:157: Film and Art Movements   Traces the growth of the "Experimental" film within the context of twentieth-century art movements; film viewings concentrate on representatives of impressionist, surrealist, futurist, new American cinema, lyrical, expanded cinema, and structural modes of filmmaking.

36B:158: Narrative and Related Art Forms

36B:160: Film Styles and Genres   Examines films in terms of various groupings; genre (for example, the western), style (for example, the New Wave) and authorship (for example, Hitchcock); topic differs from semester to semester. May be repeated.

36B:161: Film Authors   Focusing on work and vision of a single filmmaker, or comparing two or more filmmakers, course serves to intensify student's knowledge of film history, critical and analytic thinking about film.

36B:311: Influences on Film Production   Emphasis on the study of the process of film production from the point of view of the organization of the industry, the growing technology, the patterns of distribution; individual research projects.

36B:600: Seminar: American Film and American Culture   Selected American films as they reflect, shape, or illustrate relevant aspects of American culture.

36B:605: Seminar: National Cinema   Emphasis on Great Britain, Italy, Sweden, Russia, or Japan, etc.

36B:610: Seminar: Film Aesthetics and Criticism

36B:615: Seminar: Film Theory

36B:616: Seminar: Film History

Introducing Film Study in an Undergraduate Context: Queen's University*

Bill Nichols

Dept. responsible for the film program	Department of Film Studies
Full-time faculty in the dept.	4
Enrollment policies:	

Vary with specific courses (admission is to the Faculty of Arts and Sciences, not the individual department)

Staffing

% of film courses taught by part-time faculty	15%
% taught by full-time instructors or lecturers	0%
% taught by asst., assoc., and full professors	85%

Program size

# of students enrolled in the film program in fall of 1982	400 (50 majors)
# of courses offered in the fall term of 1982	9
# of courses at all levels offered in the program	14
# of students enrolled at the institution	10,000

Introduction

What follows concentrates on our introductory first-year course at Queen's University, since it is here that the central problems must be squarely faced: the relationship between filmmaking and film criticism, the identification and explanation of basic concepts in film criticism, the relation of film studies to the liberal arts generally. Preliminary to that discussion, some of the basic qualities and commitments of the Department of Film Studies should be identified in order to establish the context in which these problems have received tentative resolution.

Queen's University itself is a conservative, small-town university drawing its enrollment of ten thousand students largely from white middle- and ruling-class families. It has a solid reputation as one of Canada's best universities academically and is also somewhat notorious for its "school spirit" (whose less innocent aspects shade toward political quietism, personal complacency, and intellectual indifference—all of which pose challenges to any goals of academic excellence). The university's greatest strength lies in professional schools of law, medicine, commerce, and engineering and in selected areas of the undergraduate program. The humanities departments, although basically strong, have a few weak links, and literature and the arts are somewhat underdeveloped. Introducing questions of art and ideology is an uphill battle.

Perhaps what characterizes the film studies program most is its commitment to an understanding of both the aesthetics and ideology of film communication. This extends from lower-level courses in criticism and history to upper-year seminars in theory or special topics (such as ethnographic film or the work of Luis Buñuel) and from critical study to courses specifically devoted to film production.

Most of the department's offerings are in critical studies. Historically, the department emerged as an offshoot of the English department, and its mandate has also been posed in relation to the traditional liberal arts education of critical inquiry rather than the conservatory tradition of training individuals for careers as practicing artists. This is a mandate with which the department is entirely comfortable since this has always been understood to include the necessity for filmmaking courses. These courses provide for basic cinematic literacy—an ability to communicate in film as well as in English—and afford an opportunity for students to experiment in a tangible way with concepts issuing from a critical-studies context. Many students go on to find work in the Canadian film industry and find that their filmmaking courses combined with the opportunities for extracurricular filmmaking available here give them an adequate, if general, background. We have neither the mandate nor the desire to train technicians, craftspeople, or film artists per se. Our hope is, however, that the broad liberal arts education our graduates take with them will constitute a solid foundation upon which any of these goals—and many others for which a craft-oriented program could not prepare—can be pursued. Experience so far has borne out this hope. Nonetheless, in the future, when financial constraints are less severe, we plan to augment our filmmaking capabilities, introduce graduate study, and establish a community-oriented film or media center through which the interrelationships between art and ideology can be more extensively explored.

Faculty and Resources

At present the department's staff consists of four full-time faculty: Bill Nichols, editor of *Movies and Methods* and author of *Ideology and the Image*, whose areas of interest are semiology, systems theory, documentary and narrative film theory; Peter Morris, editor of Sadoul's *Dictionary of Film and Filmmakers* and author of *Embattled Shadows: A History of Canadian Cinema: 1895-1939*, whose areas of interest are Canadian cinema, experimental film, cross-cultural criticism, structuralism; Peter Baxter, author of *Art, Ideology and One Film: The Blue Angel* and editor of the B.F.I. anthology on Josef von Sternberg, whose areas of interest are film history, European cinema, ideology in popular culture; Peter Pearson, director of numerous documentaries and television docudramas and the feature film *Paperback Hero*, whose areas of interest are feature film directing and scripting and Canadian cultural policy. Derek Redmond, filmmaker, also teaches filmmaking on a part-time basis.

The department has Super-8 and 16mm filmmaking facilities and access to the Queen's television studio. It regularly produces films outside of a course structure through its filmmaking agency, Quarry Films. The department also has a growing archive of well over five hundred National Film Board films that the NFB has withdrawn from general circulation. The works of experimental and early Canadian filmmakers (pre-1939) are also represented. Other film holdings provide access to selected narrative and non-narrative works from various countries for research purposes. An informal departmental library supplements film books and periodicals held in the main campus library.

Course Offerings

The overall course offerings are organized in the following way. Four courses provide the core of the entire program: "Film, Culture, and Communication" (110) in the first year and three second-year courses, "Film History" (210), "Film Criticism" (220), and "Fundamentals of Film Production" (250). At the third-year level we offer the following half-year courses: "American Cinema" (300), "European Cinema" (305), "The Popular Arts in Canada" (322), "Media and Society" (330), "Women and Film" (331). Full-year courses at this level include "Advanced Film Production" (350), "Documentary Film" (365), and "Experimental Film" (375). At the fourth-year, honors level, we offer the half-year courses "Film Theory" (415), "Canadian Cinema" (e.g., NFB films from 1950-54) (422), "The Director's Cinema" (e.g., Sergei Eisenstein or Luis Buñuel) (430), "Non-Narrative Film: Special Topic" (e.g., ethnographic film) (440), "Narrative Film: Special Topic" (e.g., Japanese cinema) (445), and "Film Production: Special Topic" (e.g., documentary filmmaking) (450). Independent study and senior honors projects are also available for course credit (500/501, 510/511).

Degree Requirements

A departmental major (four-year degree) requires a student to take 110, 210, 220, 250, 415, and five and a half additional courses, of which two must be at the 300-level and one and a half at the 400-level or above.

A medial (four-year degree, split between two disciplines) requires 110, 210, 220, 250, and four additional courses, at least one of which must be at the 400-level.

A minor (three-year degree) requires 110, 210, or 220, 250, and two additional courses in film. A three-year degree requires fifteen courses in total and a four-year degree nineteen.

Planning an Introducton to Film

Several general problems confronted us in planning a first-year course. We wanted to use recent theoretizal work in film as a basis for the course, especially those writings attempting to link ideology and the cinema through its work as a system of signification. Such work signals a substantial shift in the terms of reference for film study; it promises more subtle ways of linking film and society than more traditional approaches do. Much of this work, though, is highly sophisticated and presumes a far more extensive knowledge than fourth-year students might have, let alone beginning students. It is also tendentious, and we needed to exercise great care lest some of the more farfetched theories or methodologically unpromising demonstrations burrow into the foundations of our curriculum. Nonetheless, we all felt convinced that these semiotic, psychoanalytic, structural, and Marxist currents represented a set of critical approaches that could contribute usefully to a student's knowledge, not only at advanced levels but from the very outset.

Yet we also felt that much of this recent work is exceedingly, sometimes intentionally, obscure. Without a background in nineteenth- and twentieth-century aesthetics and Marxist cultural theory, one may consider that this work often appears to be tilting at windmills, announcing "ruptures" and carrying out "interrogations" where the basic issues and larger implications remain difficult to see. Furthermore, for the most part, students do lack a background in nineteenth- and twentieth-century art and its criticism, especially in regard to popular culture. The cafeteria-style undergraduate program at Queen's (there are no required courses or areas of studies except as set by one's major department) only intensifies a problem that begins in primary and secondary school and in the politically and educationally disastrous ways in which sixties' liberalism became translated into curricular reforms (de-emphasis on writing, critical inquiry, and rigorous argument, to name a few).

A film department cannot be a student's primary source for modern history, politics, art and literature, aesthetics, semiology, structuralism, critical theory, systems theory, phenomenology, Marxism, and feminism, in addition to film theory, criticism, history, and production, yet in many cases a student's first exposure to these areas of thought comes through film study. It is ironic that despite the disparaging attitudes of some traditional humanists toward film study—as something too frivolous for serious consideration and too simple to require sophisticated methodologies—the present-day student is often ill-prepared for a successful encounter with the kind of work carried out in film study today. (Turned around, this can become an argument for making film study a specialized graduate program to pursue after acquiring more basic forms of knowledge. There is some logic to this. An undergraduate major in film may be somewhat limiting, at least from a historical perspective, but the general study of film is far too crucial to an understanding of our contemporary world to be relegated to a graduate specialty entirely. Besides, what would we do with all the humanities professors who teach the odd film course or two, often to very good effect?)

Our remedy is more than a Band-Aid but less than a complete solution. The latter requires considerable revision of our entire education system, including the questions of who goes to university and why. Partly, our remedy requires patience. One course cannot redress myriad deficiencies, but a well-thought-out departmental program can come a great deal closer to this goal. Hence we give considerable attention to the interrelationship of our courses and the overall perspective a student concentrating in film study will gain. (For example, the first-year course stresses American film, the second-year history course stresses European film, and at the third-year level half-courses in American cinema and European cinema allow for a more detailed look at one or two aspects of these two major founts of cinematic production.)

The emphasis here, though, is on our first-year course. Its current structure began to emerge through a series of department seminars in 1976–77 prompted by Guy Gauthier's article "The Semiology of the Image," obtained from the British Film Institute in photocopy form, and its accompanying slides. (The faculty at that time consisted of Nick Kendell, Jim Kitses, Joyce Nelson, and myself.) Gauthier tried to apply semiology to the still image and questions of ideology in a nonreductive but readily understandable form. Working with his paper and slide illustrations led us to a series of questions that seemed fundamental to our task: What is a text? How do we read or speak with images? How do we read or speak with motion pictures? Where does aesthetic pleasure come from? What is narrative, exposition, poetics (fiction, documentary, experimental film)? What relations pertain between art and ideology, between self and other in art and ideology? How do we address the paradoxical need to show that there is to film more than meets the eye? How, in other words, do we link systematic formal analysis with questions of social context and ideology? It also became clear that much of the recent work found in the major film magazines (*Film Quarterly, Screen, Jump Cut, Cine-Tracts, Quarterly Review of Film Studies, Cineaste,* and, while active, *Women and Film*), together with related material in nonfilm magazines and writings in ideology, cultural theory, Marxism, structuralism, psychoanalysis, and systems theory, could effectively provide the necessary conceptual framework for the course. But it would almost always need considerable recasting so that its origins and basic principles could be clearly presented to a beginning audience. This work of reformulation and integration has proved a major preoccupation for the last several years.

One grave danger is the ideology of the textbook. We regard the films screened as the primary texts and textbooks as virtual innoculations—doses of denatured analysis liable to produce an immunity to the dis-ease of rigorous and relentless criticism. Textbooks assume a nontendentious body of knowledge, of "givens" to be assimilated. (Low-angle shots "mean" power, heroism, or dominance, for example.) They are usually comfortably reductionistic, the Rolaids of cultural consumption, in which parts all "add up" harmoniously, naturally. This is not knowledge or the pursuit of knowledge—a practice inevitably involving a series of indefinite but purposeful approximations. It is ideology in the guise of the natural and obvious. (Nonetheless, student discomfort in the absence of a textbook is great. We have tended to use a text but to de-emphasize it and to encourage a skeptical distance from its generalizations. The most successful one so far, I have found, is Giannetti's *Understanding Movies*, with Thompson and Bordwell's *Film Art: An Introduction* a more precise but somewhat narrower contender. The latter is more strongly weighted toward formal analysis; it gives little attention to documentary and displaces ideology further toward the periphery. Still, its rigor is exceptional and in that it sets an exemplary model. Were I to use it I would feel more need to offer correctives to its dominant emphasis. Since I prefer not to refer to a textbook often, I have continued to use Giannetti. Monaco's *How to Read a Film* most closely approximates the course's overall structure but seems too superficial and fragmented—it lacks both the rigor of a genuine text and the imaginary unity of a "successful" textbook, though its attempt at open-endedness can only be applauded.)

As an alternative to a central textbook, our introductory course stresses lecture material and selected supplementary articles. We choose writers who are tendentious, who mark out central issues, who set the terms of debate, who openly take their stand and invite (even incite) us to argue for (or against). Examples of such materials include selections from Barthes's *Mythologies*, Sontag's *On Photography*, Dziga-Vertov's writings, Sarris' defense of American cinema and the auteur theory, Bazin's praise of neorealism or of photographic ontology, Lesage on feminist film criticism, Biskind on *On the Waterfront*, Place and Peterson on *film noir*, Michelson and Kleinhans on the avant-garde (in separate articles, of course), and Robin Wood on Hitchcock and the horror film. The greatest problem with either a textbook or articles arises from the beginning student's reluctance to read about films at all and the limited time available for discussion. At times I think we might eliminate readings altogether, but this would probably be harmful to those students who are most eager to explore.

In developing the course we have tended to isolate a few key focuses of attention in recent critical work: ideology-in-general—those forms of social representation that support our lived, everyday experience of the world (an alternative, broader definition than ideology as doctrines or rationalizations)—and the imaginary—a realm not limited to but inhabited by ideology. The imaginary centers on relations of opposition or identity, of either/or choices between self and other (the hopeless oscillation that underpins the slogan that the ego is a paranoid construct). Imaginary relationships are a necessary form of relation and support the emergence of the self-as-subject and its capacity for speech. But ideology couples with the imaginary to lock us into schizogenic or antagonistic relationships like submission/dominance and to foster our acceptance of such relationships as natural, obvious, automatic (the gut level of sexism as learned, habitual assumptions and responses by men to women as inferiors, for example, versus any clearly articulated doctrine of male supremacy). Such relations tend toward reification (making a learned process, an abstract image of women, into a concrete, material fact about women's nature), toward the stereotypic, and toward reducing relationship itself to the measure of a thing, a general equivalent such as, in our society, the phallus or money.

These are difficult concepts, but they can be explained and used, especially with the aid of copious examples. (Questions of sexism and nationalism work particularly well in the context of Queen's: sexual difference and national identity are issues that touch the center of middle- and upper-class Canadian students' lives as readily as related issues do in others'.) In fact, I introduce these ideas early in the course so that their application can be repeatedly demonstrated as we take up varying aspects of film. A summary of the lecture that does this, beginning with the psychology of perception and then moving to ideology, follows, stripped of the various examples that accompany this conceptual core.

Summary of Lecture on "Perception and the Visual World"

1. Perception is a function of an active, purposeful, socially governed activity. How does it work and how does it relate to ideology?
2. We translate a sensory array spread across the retina into a meaningful visual world. This becomes automatic: we come to recognize familiar objects in a familiar world. We may think this world is always already meaningful, but this is a deception, a function of the process' automatic nature.
3. We recognize figures against a ground extending in depth. There are gestalt "Laws of Organization" for figure recognition and "monocular depth cues" that are also used by artists and filmmakers. Ambiguous figures or depth relationships remind us of our own active involvement in making things meaningful.
4. Through these processes we begin to formulate theories or hypotheses about how the world is, what is in it, and what significance these things bear.
   a. Once formed, these theories are difficult to falsify. We make an emotional investment in how we see and tend to reject anomalous impressions rather than reject our theories or way of seeing. These theories are largely unconscious.
   b. In this regard perception is similar to other learned, sequential activities (e.g., typing, sports, speech, courtship, role playing generally). Since large components of such behavior can occur automatically, we can infer the existence of an unconscious program (or theory, or code, or habit, or way of seeing) guiding this behavior. Conversely, we can understand such behavior in general through what guides it in general—the unconscious program (the word we will use most often is "code").
5. This situation has value.
   a. It affords an economy. We need not consciously repeat routine procedures over and over.
   b. It achieves selectivity. The variety of meanings derivable from a sensory array are reduced to more singular meanings. These meanings usually reflect a cultural consensus and allow for shared perceptions and values.
6. What holds an unconscious code in place? How is it rewarded for the value it provides? Answer—that which "tells" it is working smoothly, i.e., recognition. Recognition confirms our theory, code, way of seeing. Recognition is a pleasurable experience, and this pleasure is like a dividend paid on our original emotional investment in a code, habit, or way of seeing. Such pleasure is akin to aesthetic pleasure, which tends to oscillate between recognizing the familiar and discovering the new.
7. Perception is like ideology if we consider ideology as a way of seeing the world in which we have made emotional investments. Ideology is how a society

represents itself. Ideology represents "views" that rationalize the vested interests of a society and its constituents. These views may be explicit statements, but they are more generally (representational) images, images of who we are and where we fit in the world. Ideology is the realm of imaginary relationships. As such, these views rest upon theories or codes or habits that are largely unconscious. We can't afford to question who we are at every moment.

8. For this reason ideological views are also difficult to falsify. They are at the root of our lived, customary relations to the world—of what sort of objects and other people fill it, of what relations they have to one another, of what meanings they bear for us.

9. In this sense ideology is necessary and inescapable, and necessarily unconscious. But at times we will want to gain a perspective on it, not only to live inside ideology but to understand what world this is in which we think we live.

10. What holds ideology, our life within a realm of imaginary relationships, in place? What rewards it for its consistency? Answer—the pleasure of recognition. Recognition is a dividend paid on our emotional investments in imaginary relationships, and what we gain the greatest pleasure from recognizing is an image of our self.

11. Most films and other socially produced images also represent a way of seeing the world. We often make emotional investments in them. In this sense they too are ideological. They help us recognize who we are and where we belong in the images, the views presented to us. We take pleasure in this recognition. But aesthetic pleasure also involves the discovery of the new. We may discover new possibilities for being in the world as well as recognize familiar ones.

12. One thing we will seek to discover is how films involve more than meets the eye. We'll try to appreciate the new possibilities they sometimes open up. We will also seek to understand the codes that guide their organization—those invisible, abstract, largely unconscious rules of procedure that make films what they are just as our way of seeing makes the visible world what it is.

13. We can now say that image-making (film, painting, photography, television) is an active, purposeful, socially governed activity. We can say that ideology proposes an image of who we are and what the world is like. Art, including film, does this too. Yet art is not identical with ideology. Discovering what relations exist between art and ideology will be one of the main goals of this course.

This provides the foundation for the material that follows. We can then ask in relation to particular films or types of films how they promote imaginary relationships (via the cinematic apparatus to some degree and all it hides as well as reveals, via narrative or expository structure, its techniques for displacing, condensing, and apparently resolving contradictions). How do films offer a perspective on ideology; to what degree do they put on display both the form and content of ideology? In this sense the course is clearly purposive. Its shape is guided by its purpose. Other questions could be asked, but these are the ones that seem to me the most crucial for our lives, ones we need to answer when we confront the cinema. It is asking a lot, but to ask less may amount to asking very little at all.

The sense of purpose sketched out here places the course within what Paul Ricoeur calls the school of suspicion (founded by Marx, Freud, and Nietzsche) versus the school of revelation (where he tends to locate hermeneutics and phenomenology). Exposing the ideological component to perceptual and social habits related to the cinema becomes crucial. It is often not the "Good News" motivating hermeneutics we discover but the mystifications and reifications of ideology, the motivation for suspicion. Yet suspicion does not mean constant detachment or emotional indifference. Films captivate and move us, not only ideologically but sometimes politically and aesthetically. They sometimes offer instructive pleasure that is truly revelatory and revelatory of ideology as much as anything else. They can prompt a search for alternatives to real, existing conditions and for reasons why such alternatives are absent. Films can suggest that what there is is not all there might be. But this revelation occurs within a context where aesthetics and politics cannot be fully separated. Pleasure is not innocent. Revelation is not pure. It is precisely our fascination, our captivation with and by films, that necessitates suspicion.

This is not to pit reason against emotion but to recognize that aesthetics do not exist entirely apart from ideology, on the one hand, and that our rigorous analyses are not based on experiences that fail to move us, or most of us, on the other. How we are moved—in what direction, to what end—becomes the overriding question. Without acknowledging our own captivation, for better or for worse, suspicion risks sinking into an elitist dismissal of inferior "entertainment" (as it did for most of the Frankfurt school or, more recently, most of *Screen's* contributors) or into the cynical detachment of the unaffected academic. We do, despite our best intentions—and for many, without our full awareness of alternative possibilities—invest in the circulation of images that propose imaginary relationships along class, racial, sexual, and national lines. What we need to ask is why do we settle for less than what we might imagine possible? This is not a rhetorical question. Answers are available. Marx, Freud, feminism provide many of them. These answers revolve around questions of power, material, economic, sexual, and ideology's contribution to the maintenance of power and the relations of production requiring its perpetuation—and why, even when correct analyses are available, we may continue to live within the bonds of ideology.

At a more specific level this introductory course asks how sounds and images form patterns of communication and how different patterns promote different ways of seeing (different ideological positions). What tools can the course provide to help reveal the work of film to uproot old assumptions or habits that obscure both the aesthetic and ideological effects of visual communication? The focus is upon recent mainstream cinema. Feminist, avant-garde, third world, or Godardian cinema often elicits hostile, defensive responses at first. Exposing some of the ideological implications and aesthetic subtleties of films closer to most students' previous experience provides a more comfortable starting point and arguably one of greater value to those who take no further film courses: at least they have some tools for considering the kinds of films they are most likely to see along with some awareness of the alternatives that exist.

In chronological sequence the course has the following structure:

Introduction (two weeks): responding to popular film (I often use *Singin' in the Rain*) and exploring a large, provocative area like violence and the media or the phenomenon of the spectacle.

Perception and Ideology (one week): see lecture summarized above.

The Still Image (two weeks): our positioning vis-à-vis Renaissance painting, the importance of linear perspective for the "other scene" (the place of the viewer), anchoring the potentially ambiguous meaning of images via paradigmatic, syntagmatic, and contextual relationship (i.e., the relation of what is present to what is absent but available to replace it—e.g., a fedora versus a Stetson; the relations between elements present—e.g., a man and a woman, or person and commodity; the relation of one image to another or of words [caption] to image). John Berger's film series *Ways of Seeing* has proved an invaluable aid since we began using it in 1976 even though he is probably weakest on sexism and the ideological implications of how he himself structures discussion of the nude in oil painting. (Berger's argument demonstrates the sexist assumptions behind the tradition of the nude but the form he adopts repeats at another level the very sexism he exposes.)

The Moving Image (one week): the perception of apparent motion (which is not based on persistence of vision, contrary to most textbooks), the major cinematic forms (narrative, exposition, poetics), the relations of form and content, characteristics of the cinema versus other arts.

Narrative Structure (six to seven weeks, plus seven to eight weeks in second term on selected directors, genres, national cinema): concepts of closure, of narrative codes (actions and enigmas particularly), of narrative lure and desire, the work of resolving contradictions through mechanisms like condensation, displacement, secondary revision; realism, narrative and style (via feminist filmmakers, soap opera, melodrama); the aesthetics and ideology of identification and distantiation; "postclassical" narrative.

Expository Structure (two to three weeks): direct address, rhetoric—the art of persuasiveness or courtship (including documentary, photojournalism, television news with a comparison of Canadian and U.S. broadcasts); indirect address (observational cinema and the merger of narrative and documentary forms). As with most aspects of the course, frame enlargements and extracts are extensively used. Placing material in a new context helps disclose some of its implications and encourages a sense that images can be confronted actively and not simply absorbed passively.

Poetic Structure (two weeks): the experience of form, experimentation with form, cinematic analysis of the cinematic experience (e.g., Paul Sharits' and David Rimmer's work), formal qualities of motion pictures as sources of content and form.

The Cinematic Context (seven to eight weeks): genre (one selected from western, musical, gangster, *film noir*—which I do not consider a genre but related to that concept in interesting ways), auteur (usually a European like Bergman or Bertolucci, and Alfred Hitchcock, who receives three weeks' attention as a subject from which to summarize much of the course's content), national cinema (Hollywood, Canadian cinema, and the "North American" syndrome); the third world cinema.

Because one goal is to invite students to become active, engaged, critically aware users of visual communication, there is a necessary integration of film theory and practice. Written papers are set (and evaluated in individual conferences), but so are visual-aural exercises. These provide a "hands-on" component that erases the sense of passive consumption and introduces a feeling for what the actual fabrication of patterns of sound and moving images is like. No technical skills beyond using a simple Super-8 camera are taught. Our total supply of equipment is six Super-8 cameras. Students supply whatever else is needed on their own. These exercises include:

Super-8 Film Project: Choose a subject, then using one cassette shoot half the roll in a long take and the other half by editing in the camera. Projects are shown to the entire class and discussed in tutorial. (This helps give a sense of screen time, the frame, mise-en-scène, composition, associations between shots, etc.)

Slide Project: Study the films of Alfred Hitchcock shown in class (e.g., *Suspicion, Notorious, North by Northwest, The Birds, Psycho*) and the storyboard examples in *Focus on Hitchcock*. Using a 36-roll of slide film, shoot series of stills to represent the shots that would form a narrative sequence in the style of Alfred Hitchcock. (These are shown and discussed the same way as the film projects. Certain tendencies, e.g., misogyny, are often discussed in advance to encourage careful consideration of a theme. Helps give a sense of storyboarding, narrative structure, continuity editing, emotional impact in relation to formal or stylistic choices.)

Sound Project: Prepare a two- to five-minute cassette investigating some aspect of Canadian culture and exploring the possibilities of sound. (Helps students explore possible relations among words, music, sound effects. Projects can explore any aspect of culture and frequently take students into the field for research, e.g., interviews. This also proves the most difficult project since many students have trouble seeing what they can do with sound that is imaginative.)

This gives some general impression of how we try to introduce film study. Discussion of the individual films shown each week plays a crucial role, but lectures and discussion also try to make clear the elements common to various forms of visual communication (painting, photography, television, film) and their uses. They especially try to elaborate on the complex set of relationships pertaining between ideology and the image—not only in the general way that such a summary necessitates but in exacting detail as we examine specific images and particular films. It is a course that, from the available indicators, has worked well in its own context and may, we hope, stimulate thought along similar lines elsewhere.

Note

*A version of this essay appeared in *Jump Cut* nos. 24–25 (1981): 53–56.

Queen's University

Enrollment

All film courses except 110, 210, and 220 have a limited enrollment. Students are required to obtain permission of the instructor to register.

Prerequisites

Unless otherwise specified under individual course descriptions, the prerequisite for 300-level film courses is one previous film course or permission of the department; for 400-level film courses, prerequisites are two previous film courses or permission of the department.

Language Requirements

There are no formal language requirements for study of the cinema, but students intending to complete a concentration in film studies are encouraged to acquire a working knowledge of French. This is particularly advisable in the light of the major critical and creative contributions of France to the world of film. A knowledge of French is also useful for the study of Canadian cinema, since many French-Canadian films are available in the original version only, without English titles.

Bachelor of Arts, Minor Concentration: Film 110, 210 or 220, 250, two additional courses in film.

Bachelor of Arts (Honors), Major Concentration: Film 110, 210, 220, 250, 415, five and one-half additional courses in film, at least two of which must be at the 300-level and one and one-half at the 400-level or above.

Medial Concentration: Film 110, 210 or 220, 250, four additional courses in film, at least one of which must be at the 400-level.

Courses

34-110: Film, Culture, and Communication   A basic introduction to the cinema. The aesthetic and ideological significance of visual communication together with the specific qualities of the film form provide the main focus for the course. Emphasis falls upon a wide range of contemporary filmmaking with some attention given to television, advertising, and photography. Course work includes both written and cinematic exercises.

34-210: History of Film   The study of film in a historical, sociocultural context with emphasis on historical analysis and research methods. Particular styles, conventions, movements, genres, and film artists are selected for close study.

34-220: Film Criticism   Drawing on selected examples of fiction, documentary, and experimental film, the course surveys basic critical approaches to film such as genre, auteur, formal, and political criticism in order to provide a sound basis for the appreciation and analysis of various kinds of filmmaking.

34-250: Fundamentals of Film Production   In addition to individual film projects, a series of group projects is undertaken in order to provide a grounding in basic filmmaking techniques. The course includes work in Super-8 and 16mm, sound recording and videotaping. Prerequisite: Film 110.

34-300: American Cinema   A framework for concentrated study in the Hollywood cinema, this course may focus on a particular director, genre, star, era, studio. By looking systematically at a specific aspect of Hollywood, the course seeks to illuminate the dialectic of forces—artistic, industrial, social—within which the classical Hollywood movie developed.

34-305: European Cinema   Close study of selected films and directors from major European film-production countries. The course focuses upon questions of style, meaning, and evaluation in a cross-cultural context.

34-322: The Popular Arts in Canada   With an emphasis upon the Canadian film industry, the course examines the social, historical, and economic nature of the popular arts and mass media in Canada. The influence of other cultures upon Canada's is also treated. Prerequisite: A previous film course is desirable, but the course is open without prerequisite to students completing a concentration in a related area.

34-330: Media and Society   Although films are often seen simply as entertainment products or as works of art, they clearly play a larger cultural and social role. This course examines the way in which cinema can be related to the preoccupations of societies at particular historical moments by exploring the ideological and/or historical implications of selected film styles. Prerequisite: Although a previous film course is desirable, this course is open without prerequisite to students completing a concentration in a related area.

34-331: Women and Film The cinema's treatment of women may suggest otherwise, but the medium has not always been in the hands of men. Through the analysis of specific film examples, this course examines the ways in which women filmmakers from a variety of countries have used the cinema to explore their consciousness and alter or challenge social stereotypes. This course also attempts to deal with problems involved in developing a feminist aesthetic. Prerequisite: Permission of the instructor.

34-350: Advanced Film Production Fall Term: An intensive workshop-seminar focusing on a series of practical exercises and script proposals. The exercises provide a grounding in 16mm camera use, lighting, sound, editing, and directing. Winter Term: Selected script proposals are filmed as class projects and taken through the final mixing stage. Prerequisite: Film 250. Enrollment is limited to fifteen students.

34-365: Documentary Film An examination of the various styles, aims, and methods of the documentary approach to filmmaking. Special reference is made to the contribution of Canadian filmmakers (including the work of the National Film Board). Offered in alternate years.

34-375: The Experimental Film An introduction to the nature and range of the experimental tradition in the cinema. While surveying origins and early movements, such as the French avant-garde of the twenties, the course places a special weight on the development of the contemporary independent movement centered in the work of figures such as Brakhage, Anger, Warhol, Snow, Rimmer, Mekas. Offered in alternate years. Prerequisite: Film 110. Prerequisite or Corequisite: Film 210 or 220.

34-415: Film Theory An inquiry into the historical development and current state of film theory. Emphasis is on the critical analysis of written texts that explore film's relationship to reality and to the spectator, film as a semiotic system, film's ideological functions, and principles of narrative and formal structure in film. Prerequisites: Film 110, 220, and admission to honors.

34-422: Canadian Cinema An intensive examination of a particular aspect of the Canadian cinema. Topics such as Canadian film history, the study of one or two directors, the questions of regionalism in Canadian film, of a Canadian film aesthetic, or a comparison of French and English Canadian filmmaking provide the precise focus. Prerequisites: Film 110, 220. Prerequisite or Corequisite: Film 322.

34-430: The Director's Cinema Study in depth of the body of work of selected major filmmakers. This course is both an application of this particular critical method—the idea of the film author—and an investigation of its value and limitations. Prerequisites: Film 110, 210 or 220, 300 or 305.

34-440: Non-Narrative Film: Special Topic Concentrated study of selected aspects of the documentary or experimental movements. Focus may be on the work of a particular filmmaker or on stylistic and critical problems posed by the non-narrative film. Prerequisites: Film 110 and 220. Prerequisite or Corequisite: Film 365 and/or 375.

34-445: Narrative Film: Special Topic Concentrated study of selected aspects of the narrative film. Problems of critical analysis or historiography introduced at an earlier level are examined in greater detail in association with a selected area of focus. Prerequisites: Film 110, 220, 300 or 305.

34-450: Film Production: Special Topic   The course focuses upon a particular form of filmmaking (documentary, experimental, animation, narrative) in any given year. Students work on a major project in small groups, drawing upon existing examples of the particular form in question and emphasizing the refinement of artistic skills. Prerequisite: Film 250. Enrollment is limited to fifteen students.

34-500, -501: Senior Project in Film   Third-year students completing a major or medial concentration in film studies are encouraged to submit an application to the department for an independent senior project or thesis in a selected area of film studies. Applications should be made before the end of the third year and the applicant must satisfy the department that he or she is sufficiently knowledgeable about the areas selected to undertake the project.

34-510, 511: Independent Study Project   Students may arrange a program of selected study in consultation with members of the department. Prerequisite: Admission to honors.

PART II

SELECTED PROGRAM DESCRIPTIONS

The Interdisciplinary Film Studies Program at Bowling Green State University

Jack Nachbar

Dept. responsible for the film program	Program is run by several departments in
the College of Arts and Sciences.	
Full-time faculty in the dept.	about 10
Enrollment policies	
maximum class enrollment (if applicable)	N/A
minimum class enrollment	N/A
average class enrollment	20–50
Staffing	
% of film courses taught by part-time faculty	20%
% taught by full-time instructors or lecturers	10%
% taught by asst., assoc., and full professors	70%
Program size	
# of students enrolled in the film program in	
fall of 1981	360 (15 majors, 15 minors)
# of courses offered in the fall term of 1981	10
# of courses at all levels offered in the program	35
# of students enrolled at the institution	15,000

Located in a small Ohio town at least ninety minutes from any urban center that regularly screens quality films and with most of its undergraduates majoring in business and education, Bowling Green State University is quite unlikely ever to enjoy a reputation as a hotbed of movie mania. Student interest in films is confined for the most part to recent commercial hits. As a result, little inner university political pressure in favor of films can be brought to bear because administrators are reluctant to spend increasingly precious dollars on activities in low demand. Despite these problems, a formal curriculum in film studies is alive and well at Bowling Green. This has been accomplished by the quite logical step of minimizing costs by creating a program in film studies that employs the interests and expertise of faculty and students from several university departments and schools. Because there is not enough interest in film to justify the creation of a separate department, the Bowling Green faculty works cooperatively within a program that is totally interdisciplinary.

During the winter of 1975 the dean of the College of Arts and Sciences invited interested faculty within the college to form an ad hoc committee charged with the duties of bringing better organization to film studies courses on campus and deciding if it was possible to structure a film studies major and minor based mainly on preexisting courses. Faculty from English, foreign languages, history, philosophy, and popular culture departments and the radio-tv-film program accepted the dean's invitation and began to attend weekly meetings. By the following fall it had been decided that a film studies program was indeed feasible if some additional courses were added to those already offered both inside and outside the college. A film studies program proposal subsequently made the rounds of various campus committees and was finally approved and operable by the fall of 1977.

Two educational assumptions have determined the form of the program, both as it was originally developed by the committee and as it has evolved since its initial implementation.

The Film Studies Program Must Reflect the Values and Traditions of the Liberal Arts Curriculum.

Because the location of film studies was within the College of Arts and Sciences, all the members of the original committee agreed that a program in film should reflect the general education, liberal arts orientation of university studies that the arts and sciences have traditionally represented and espoused. Film study would betray the traditional mission of the college if it were a narrowly focused program emphasizing only the production, history, and aesthetics of film itself. Instead, the committee devised a plan intended to broaden the context of film understanding by keeping the courses in traditional liberal arts disciplines and by demanding that students enroll in courses from as many of these disciplines as possible. Ideally, students emerge from such a group of courses knowledgeable about film but also enriched by contact with literature, foreign cultures, and philosophy as well.

To ensure this traditional liberal arts objective of a "well-rounded" education, the committee did two things: it established a permanent interdisciplinary structure for the program and created a broadly based core of courses for film studies students.

The committee first of all decided for the good of the program not to place it under the control of an established department. An independent film studies program ensures the broad, liberal arts experience for film students by maintaining a balance of power between contributing disciplines. All program policy is determined by the Film Studies Committee, which has become an official standing committee of the college. This committee is made up of one member from each department in the college that regularly offers at least one course on film. A program director, responsible for academic advising and general administration, is selected by the dean of the college among the members of the committee. His or her appointment is subject to periodical review and renewal.

Students majoring in film studies begin their programs by selecting eight courses from the following list:

Core Courses

Understanding Movies (radio-tv-film). How films communicate.

History and Criticism of Film (radio-tv-film). An international history.

Introduction to Popular Film (popular culture). Hollywood industry as mythmaker for the masses.

Literature and Film (English). Comparison of techniques employed in each medium.

One course in foreign film:

Cultural and Literary Aspects of German Film (German). Variable topics.

Cultural and Literary Aspects of Soviet Film (Russian). Variable topics.

European and Latin American Cinema (Romance languages). Variable topics.

The Italian Cinema (Italian).

One course in photography:

Introduction to Photojournalism (journalism).

Introduction to Photography (visual communications technology).

Super-8 Filmmaking (radio-tv-film).

16mm Filmmaking (radio-tv-film).

One upper-division course in thematic studies:

Seminar: Contemporary Aspects of Broadcasting and Film (radio-tv-film) (when film related).

Advanced Studies in Popular Film (popular culture). Variable topics—usually a popular genre.

Studies in Literature and Film (English). Variable topics.

Philosophy of Film (philosophy). Filmmakers' approaches to basic philosophical problems.

The program adviser helps each student plan core courses and encourages him or her to sample from as many disciplines as possible. When the typical student completes the core he or she will have taken courses in film history, film as a comparative medium, film aesthetics, and film production. Equally important is that the same student will have been introduced to the methods and ideas of radio-tv-film, English, philosophy, a foreign culture, and journalism.

The Film Studies Program Must Be Flexible.

In constructing the film studies curriculum, the committee realized the necessity of being practical as well as idealistic. As a state university, Bowling Green serves students who are motivated to attend college primarily because they want training for a career. Although adamant about maintaining film studies within the liberal arts, the committee devised a second set of courses under each of two tracks designed to provide students with a vocational plan of studies.

Creative-Technical Track
The creative-technical track is provided for those students who are primarily interested in the production of films. Students electing this emphasis must take nineteen semester hours (approximately seven courses) in addition to the twenty-four hours required by the core curriculum. The track is composed of a selection of film, theater, television, journalism, and photography courses taught in the schools of Art, Industrial Education and Technology, Journalism, and Speech Communication. These courses provide a strong background in visual communication skills and allow for individual interests in areas such as photography, lighting, acting, and directing.

radio-tv-film: Introduction to Television Program Production, Producing and Directing for TV, Problems in Film (Advanced Film Projects).
theater: Principles of Acting, Stagecraft, Directing, Advanced Directing, Stage Lighting, Theatrical Costuming, Playwriting.
journalism: Introduction to Photojournalism, Photographic Communication, Color Photography, The Documentary.
art: Creative Photography.
visual communications technology: Visual Communications Technology, Photography II, Animation Technology.

History-Theory-Criticism Track
The purpose of the history-theory-criticism track is to provide the student with an understanding of the role of film in modern society. Through an integrated series of courses in the liberal arts, the student examines film both as a distinctive art form and as a historical document reflecting the values and attitudes of the society in which it was created. Students electing this emphasis must take nineteen semester hours (approximately seven courses) in addition to the twenty-four hours required by the core curriculum.

English: Literature and Film; Writing about Film (writing both reviews and analytical film criticism). Studies in Literature and Film,* Writing Film Criticism.
history: Europe in the Modern World: An Experiment in History through Film (films as expressions of the era and milieu in which they were made). Special Studies in History (when film-related).
philosophy: Philosophy of Film.
popular culture: Advanced Studies in Popular Film,* Studies in the History of American Popular Film* (variable topics, each on a specific era of American film history).

Romance languages: European and Latin American Cinema.*
Italian: The Italian Cinema.
German: Cultural and Literary Aspects of German Film.*
Russian: Cultural and Literary Aspects of Soviet Film.*
radio-tv-film: Seminar: Contemporary Aspects of Broadcasting and Film (when film-related).

*Courses thus marked may be repeated once if topics are different.

Unlike the core of courses, neither of the tracks includes specific, required courses. Each student works closely with the film studies adviser in planning a set of courses that will meet that individual's needs and goals. A student interested in writing as a career, for example, would select the history-theory-criticism track. Within this track, a student would mainly choose writing courses in English and study film as a mass medium in popular culture. A student who wished to live in Europe, on the other hand, might well take most of his or her courses in foreign language films.

Despite the vocational orientation of the tracks, the goal of a liberal education is still partially met. Students must select courses from several widely diverse departments. Ten departments and schools from three colleges currently offer courses that are included in the film studies program. In either track, students enroll in courses from at least four of them.

Problems and Successes

The problem of campus political indifference that pushed the film studies program into its interdisciplinary structure in the first place continues to be the program's central frustration. In a time of tight academic money, for example, the administration cannot afford to increase the film studies budget, most of which is redistributed to departments on a matching basis for the purchase or rental of films used in film courses. This lack of adequate funding has meant that courses have had to compromise their syllabi and show fewer movies. In addition, this means the university currently lacks needed equipment such as Steenbeck tables that would enable students to study individual films with the proper intensity. These limitations in turn have meant a slow growth pattern in film studies majors and minors. Although the number of majors had increased slightly each year, by the end of 1981 there were only about fifteen. Several potential film studies majors have transferred to the School of Speech Communication to concentrate on television production because the number of film production courses is too small and no substantive funding will be available in the near future for either the updating of film production facilities or the hiring of film production instructors.

Despite the lack of resources for the adequate study of film, since the implementation of the film studies program the film environment at Bowling Green has improved significantly. The number of courses on film, for example, has more than doubled during the last four years. All the courses on foreign film, the upper-level courses in English and popular culture, and the Super-8mm and "Understanding Movies" courses offered by the radio-tv-film program were initially developed for the purpose of contributing a needed component to film studies.

And because there are more courses offered, more students elect to take them. Almost three times as many students per year (almost 900) take film courses now than took them in 1976.

The film studies program has also had an effect outside of the classroom. There are currently, for example, at least two annual week-long foreign film festivals at Bowling Green. These are cosponsored and cofinanced by the foreign language departments and the film studies program. Members of the Film Studies Committee have also helped develop an annual student film festival. Other members of the committee have directed the conversion of an old classroom into a film theater suitable for both classroom and public film showings. The film studies program has been awarded its first endowed scholarship by Lillian Gish. And, finally, the program has noticeably improved the spirit of campus cooperation in matters relating to film. In the fall of 1980, for example, a course in science fiction films was offered to sixty students by the Department of Popular Culture. Part of the instruction was done by a member of the Department of Philosophy, and most of the rental costs for the films were paid for by the Student Activities Film Committee, which also showed the films to the campus at large.

The film studies program at Bowling Green State University has yet to prove if it can attract and serve large numbers of eager film majors and minors. Nevertheless, members of the Film Studies Committee remain convinced that the interdisciplinary approach they have developed is a worthwhile addition to the liberal arts curriculum at a university that cannot afford significant new funding of liberal arts courses. And they are happy that their cooperative efforts are inducing even the vocationally oriented students of Bowling Green to see, study, and enjoy better and more varied films.

The Major in Film Studies

> Radio-TV-Film 261: Understanding Movies. How films communicate. (3 credits)
> Radio-TV-Film 466: History and Criticism of Film. An international history. (3 credits)
> Popular Culture 250: Introduction to Popular Film. Hollywood industry as mythmaker for the masses. (3 credits)
> English 200: Literature and Film. Comparison of techniques employed in each medium. (3 credits)
> One course in foreign film:
>> German 415: Cultural and Literary Aspects of German Film. Variable topics. (3 credits)
>> Russian 415: Cultural and Literary Aspects of Soviet Film. Variable topics. (3 credits)
>> Romance Languages 200: European and Latin American Cinema. Variable topics. (3 credits)
>> Italian 261: The Italian Cinema. (3 credits)
> One course in photography:
>> Journalism 306: Introduction to Photojournalism. (3 credits)
>> Visual Communications Technology 282: Introduction to Photography. (3 credits)
> Radio-TV-Film 264: Super-8 Filmmaking. (3 credits)

Radio-TV-Film 464: 16mm Filmmaking. (3 credits)

One upper-division course in thematic studies:

Radio-TV-Film 469: Seminar: Contemporary Aspects of Broadcasting and Film (when film-related). (3 credits)

Popular Culture 350: Advanced Studies in Popular Film. Variable topics: usually a popular genre. (3 credits)

English 385: Studies in Literature/Film. Variable topics. (3 credits)

Philosophy 335: Philosophy of Film. Filmmakers' approaches to basic philosophical problems. (3 credits)

Nineteen hours (seven courses) in either a creative-technical track or a history-theory-criticism track (courses in either track to be selected by the student).

The Minor in Film Studies

Radio-TV-Film 261: Understanding Movies. (3 credits)

Radio-TV-Film 464: 16mm Filmmaking. (3 credits)

Speech 466: History and Criticism of Film. (3 credits)

English 200: Literature and Film. (3 credits)

Popular Culture 250: Introduction to Popular Film. (3 credits)

One course in foreign film:

German 415: Cultural and Literary Aspects of German Film. (3 credits)

Russian 415: Cultural and Literary Aspects of Soviet Film. (3 credits)

Romance Languages 200: European and Latin American Cinema. (3 credits)

One course in photography:

Journalism 306: Introduction to Photojournalism. (3 credits)

Visual Communications Technology 282: Introduction to Photography. (3 credits)

One upper-division course in thematic studies:

Radio-TV-Film 469: Contemporary Aspects of Broadcasting and Film (when film-related). (3 credits)

Popular Culture 350: Advanced Studies in Popular Film. (3 credits)

English 385: Studies in Literature and Film. (3 credits)

Philosophy 335: Philosophy of Film (recommended). (3 credits)

The Film Program at Western Illinois University

Janice R. Welsch

Dept. responsible for the film program   Department of English

Full-time faculty in the dept.   46

Enrollment policies

    maximum class enrollment (if applicable)   N/A

    minimum class enrollment   for 200-level: 15; for 300- and 400-levels: 10

    average class enrollment   for 200-level: 40; for 300- and 400-levels: 20

Staffing

    % of film courses taught by part-time faculty   0%

    % taught by full-time instructors or lecturers   0%

    % taught by asst., assoc., and full professors   100%

Program size

    # of students enrolled in the film program in fall of 1981   300

    # of courses offered in the fall term of 1981   4

    # of courses at all levels offered in the program   10

    # of students enrolled at the institution   10,000

The introductory course (English 290) is offered each semester, usually in six sections of approximately forty students each.

Western Illinois University, situated in a rural community of west central Illinois, draws approximately sixty percent of its ten thousand students from Chicago and its suburbs. Most other students come from small towns and rural areas of the state. Having originated as a normal school, the university still provides training for a large number of education majors; other disciplines of notable strength include business, health sciences, and law enforcement, areas associated with current employment opportunities. Students are generally from middle- and working-class families and view their college education primarily as job training rather than education per se.

The film minor program at Western Illinois University was initiated in 1978 after it became apparent that the ten existing film courses being offered at the university, if brought together as an interdisciplinary unit, could provide interested students with a sound introduction to the art of the cinema. The courses reflect the concerns of four departments within two colleges. In the College of Arts and Sciences three departments offer eight film courses: "Introduction to Film," "Film History" I and II, "Film and Literature," and "Film Criticism" are English department courses; "Film and Television Documentary" and "Film and the Public Interest" are available in the Department of Communication Arts and Sciences; and "Politics and the Cinema" is a political science course. Two production courses— "Basic Motion Picture Photography" and "Motion Picture Production"—are offered by Learning Resources within the College of Education.

These offerings have been organized into two film minors: a general minor that requires the satisfactory completion of six of the film courses and allows students to concentrate exclusively on history and criticism or to include film production in their program and a minor for teacher education majors requiring eight film courses that encompass criticism, history, and production. The introductory film course and the two history courses are required for both minors.

Individually and collectively the courses aim to encourage, deepen, and extend student interest in and knowledge of films as an art and as a communication medium. Generally, students have seen many feature fiction movies, documentaries, and educational films, but they are often unaware of film techniques or of how individual films work, the multiple contexts in which they can be read, and the variety of critical approaches that can lead to greater insight and enjoyment. They may react strongly to specific movies or to certain elements within movies without understanding that their responses have been consciously elicited by filmmakers who have manipulated their material to precise effect. Though casually familiar with films representing different eras, styles, genres, and, in some cases, countries, our students commonly are not acquainted with the historical development or evolution of various film styles and genres or of the industry itself. The political uses to which film has been put, the processes and skills required to make a film, and the relationship of film to other arts are largely unknown. Through the courses that make up the film program, these varied concerns are addressed.

Underlying all the teaching involved in the film program is the attempt to develop or deepen students' critical perception of what they see and hear, to help them not only see and hear more but analyze intelligently what they view. The filmmaker D. W. Griffith put it quite succinctly: "The task I'm trying to achieve is above all to make you see." Seeing involves understanding as well as observation, an appreciation of technique as well as of content and context. This seems to be particularly important in contemporary society, where visual media have come to play important, multiple roles in the lives of many people. Not only have films been accorded the status of fine art and given the serious attention received by other aesthetically enriching and humanizing arts, but they also have been recognized, even more extensively, as a popular art and major leisure activity accessible through television and in theaters. Like other forms of popular art, films reflect and reinforce the needs, values, and desires of society. In addition, motion pictures have been utilized in many educational situations, their visual impact strengthening the verbal instruction and information being given, lending force and immediacy to a particular position being argued, or providing a point of departure for discussion and action. With film so widely available, visual literacy is a definite asset; it is an objective in each of the courses offered within the scope of the film minor.

Each course focuses on the filmmaking process and the film product within a discipline that provides specific perspectives (aesthetic, historical, ideological, sociological, technical) from which to view motion pictures. The intent is not simply to deepen the students' critical appreciation but also to broaden it through these diverse approaches and the introduction of types of films the students have not seen previously, such as foreign and avant-garde films. This effort to extend the scope of students' visual acuity is enhanced by the interdisciplinary nature of the film minor since it mirrors cinema's various facets and uses. The criticism and history courses offered by the English department are taught chiefly by professors whose graduate work has been in cinema, while the personnel teaching the film courses in other departments have made this field an adjunct to their primary areas of study. As a result, methodologies as well as content emphases differ, providing students with multiple points of view from which to see movies. Having the courses concentrated in a separate, independent department with professors whose specializations are in film theory, criticism, history, genres, and production could also achieve breadth as well as depth of exposure. Since the WIU courses constitute a minor rather than a major program, however, the interdisciplinary approach is appropriate. This would be true whether or not the program arose from existing courses, but it would not be true if all those involved had degrees in disciplines other than cinema and no one provided students with a specifically cinematic orientation to this eclectic art.

Recognizing film as a medium of communication and of record as well as a visual and narrative art makes possible its alignment with many disciplines: broadcasting, political science, anthropology, education, language, fine arts, literature, and even business. The film minor complements students in these diverse fields by giving students who choose to study film a solid basis for effectively incorporating and utilizing it in their principal area of study and for enriching their exploration of the arts. For education majors interested in teaching film studies who are also studying a certifiable discipline, the minor provides a thorough and formal introduction to motion-picture production and criticism. Should they be asked to teach film to grade or high school students, they have the knowledge and the resources to do so.[1] The minor also offers the necessary background to students planning to pursue graduate film studies.

The emphasis on film's interdisciplinary connections and its pragmatic use within a number of occupations developed when the film program was presented to college and university committees as part of the justification for the film minor.

Within the individual courses, however, the primary focus is on specific films and the techniques, history, criticism, and theory that emanate from the works themselves. How movies can enhance and serve other disciplines is pointed out, but film utility is not stressed. How films work and how we can read them on a variety of levels inevitably become the focal points of the discussions triggered by the weekly film screenings scheduled as part of each course.

In "Introduction to Film" students study experimental and documentary as well as American and foreign feature fiction movies. Hollywood features are the central focus of the course, however. They are explored in terms of film techniques and film style, genre and auteur criticism, the commercial film industry, fine and popular art, and national cinemas. Two lecture-discussions follow each week's film showing. Usually the first centers on the film itself, aided at times by a re-screening of key scenes; the second goes beyond the film while using it to initiate a study of lighting, camera movement, *film noir*, westerns, or other general film topics. An attempt is made to lead students to an awareness of the relationship between the techniques chosen and the ideas expressed in each film and also to provide them with guidelines for doing their own analyses of any film they see.

In the history courses the primary focus is again feature fiction, though more foreign countries are represented in the films selected for study. Film history students are expected to be familiar with film techniques, but these are sometimes isolated to help identify national cinemas and trends in styles. Lectures emphasize the films' aesthetic, ideological, political, and social contexts. As in the introductory course, however, initial discussion includes any aspect of a film that aids our understanding of the individual work. Recognized classics are seen and discussed along with lesser-known films that illustrate particular historical developments within the industry and the art.

Lectures and discussions in "Film Criticism" concentrate on the multiple approaches that have been and are being used to illuminate the work of filmmakers. Theoretical and historical background includes the presentation of the formalist and realist positions, discussions of the emergence and development of auteur and genre criticism, and analysis of sociological and psychological readings of films. Examinations of more recent critical approaches—structuralist, semiological, Marxist, and feminist—round out this course. Here, too, weekly film screenings provide the core around which discussions and lectures revolve. Using particular films as springboards to even the most abstract concepts provides students with a common experience from which to test hypotheses and correctly places film art before film theory.

Frequently "Film and Literature" is taught as an adaptation course with emphasis on the unique as well as shared characteristics of novels, short stories, plays, and films; specific literary and dramatic works are studied in their original and adapted forms. In other instances the course is organized thematically. Under the subtitle "Images of Men and Women in Film and Short Stories," for example, various traditional, transitional, and contemporary character depictions are studied within the contexts of the particular literary and cinematic works in which they appear. Initiated to avoid the superficial comparisons and evaluations students so easily fall into when studying an original work and its adaptation, the thematic approach has continued because of its flexibility and the favorable responses of both teachers and students. When possible the course is team-taught with specialists in film and literature assigning weekly films and short stories and taking primary responsibility for the discussions in their area of expertise. Whether team-taught or not, guest lecturers are brought in to give pertinent historical, mythic, and literary contexts through which the relatedness as well as the distinctiveness of individual stories and films can be more fully appreciated.

In "Politics and the Cinema" the propaganda potential of film is extensively investigated, and movies about governmental leadership and about national and international conflicts are studied. Other questions considered are the impact on subject matter of the political climate at the time of a film's production and the advantages and disadvantages of presenting political issues in both fictional and documentary movies. In "Film and Television Documentary" a historical exploration of documentary films and video tapes is conducted, with emphasis on their social utility and impact and their informational and propagandistic uses. Some time is spent on the technical developments that have influenced the documentary, but the course is essentially an analytical overview of the product itself. "Film and the Public Interest," like the documentary course, encompasses television as well as movies; it focuses primarily on motion-picture and television regulation. The development, objectives, implications, and mechanisms of regulation are examined in the light of the social, political, and aesthetic factors influencing films' content and exhibition.

Other courses in criticism and aesthetics that have been discussed in relation to the film minor include "Film Music" and "Experimental Film," the former to be taught by a professor of music, the latter to be team-taught by faculty from the art and English departments. Also under discussion is a seminar for teachers and education majors that would cover much of the material presented in "Introduction to Film," but with emphasis on adaptation to elementary and secondary classes and some consideration of the practical aspects of teaching film. Additionally, a sequence of 16mm unit film production courses to be offered by the art department has actually been included in the WIU undergraduate catalog for several years but awaits implementation. If this happens, the courses would augment those currently available through Learning Resources.

The objective of Learning Resources' "Basic Motion Picture Photography" and "Motion Picture Production" is to help students acquire the practical knowledge and skill necessary to make motion pictures that are effective communication tools. Emphasis during the preliminary course is on preplanning and shooting, though students are also given instruction in basic editing procedures. In the follow-up course the skills already learned are sharpened and expanded, more time is given to editing, and techniques of sound production are explored and utilized. Though previously taught using 16mm cameras, both courses are currently using Super-8 equipment because of the high cost of 16mm filmmaking. Such budget-related limitations are particularly evident in this area, but all the film criticism and history courses are also affected by budgetary restrictions.

The cost associated with a film program is perhaps the most crucial practical consideration both administrators and teachers must face when setting the perimeters of such a program. To be able to present films that are appropriate to each week's topics while remaining within a limited budget calls for considerable ingenuity as well as a willingness to compromise when necessary. Acquaintance with the college sales representatives of the 16mm film distributors and some ability to negotiate favorable rental rates have resulted in an increase in the quality and/or quantity of films made available by those distributors; though this usually entails selecting a minimum of five or six films from a single source, the benefits have outweighed the restrictions involved. Cooperation among the professors teaching film, enabling two or more classes to be brought together for a single screening that fits the schedule of each class, has also been a way of stretching the film rental budget. This not only has demanded planning, and perhaps compromise, by the teachers but also has necessitated coordination of class times and room assignments.

Indirectly the departmental film budget has been supplemented further by incorporating one or two movies offered by other campus organizations into class viewing schedules. These extracurricular screenings, along with appropriate commercial shows, also provide the material for critical papers assigned in film history and criticism classes. Other options pursued to control the cost of film analysis courses without cutting the number of films shown are the acquisition of a library of film classics and membership in a consortium of colleges and universities that share films that have been jointly leased or purchased. Of course, increased access to the films that these options permit and the budgetary gains involved must be weighed against the more limited number of titles available to us.

Further practical considerations that are unique in scope within humanities courses revolve around the facilities and equipment needed for the successful projection of movies. To be adequate, facilities must provide comfortable seating for the students and must be equipped with a projection system and a sound system that permit students to see without distortion and to hear without strain. For the in-depth analysis of motion pictures it would be a boon to have at one's disposal not only regular projectors but also one that can advance or reverse film frame by frame and that can be stopped on a single frame. Also desirable are film viewers, such as a flatbed viewer, that enable one to study closely camera movement and elements of the mise-en-scène. Though this equipment is not available to us, we have been able to do close analysis of a few films with the aid of a laser disc player available through the audiovisual center of the WIU library. At present, the videodisc system seems to be our only option for detailed study of shots and scenes.

Budgets, equipment and facilities, film scheduling and projection may be the most basic aspects of the film program, but other practical facets are of more interest. One such item, also ultimately related to budgetary considerations, is the popularity of film study. At WIU the introductory course consistently draws about 250 students per semester. Average enrollment for each of the other criticism courses is twenty-five while the production courses regularly attract the fifteen-student limit. The departments offering these film courses have benefited through the increased credit-hour production resulting from the relatively large enrollments. This positive student response has been most helpful in justifying the expense of film rentals and equipment, particularly in the English department where enrollments and the numbers of majors have diminished in recent years as a greater proportion of students turn to disciplines that more immediately and clearly lead to employment.

Seen from an administrative point of view, the high enrollment in the introductory course is impressive. From the perspective of the instructor of the course, however, student participation is not totally positive. Genuine interest or curiosity about film motivates some students, but others initially view the course as an easy three credits in humanities that will help fulfill basic curriculum requirements. More interested students enroll in the upper-level courses, but even these students usually have seen few films other than Hollywood features. Much film teaching within the program, therefore, is very basic. It provides a solid foundation in the art, but each course is, in effect, a survey course, and the program as a whole is an introductory program. It serves the needs of the students at WIU by sharpening their awareness of how film works and suggesting the many ways films can enhance other disciplines, while guiding students to develop their analytical and critical abilities.

Note

[1] The need to prepare prospective educators to teach film classes in elementary and secondary schools seems to have been first recognized by teachers in social studies, English, and other subjects who have been asked to do just that without any formal introduction to film study. Many have done an admirable job of preparing themselves, but we should by now be aware of the vacuum that exists and help future interested teachers prepare as fully and effectively as possible. Perhaps with greater recognition and support on the university level, film study will be more readily accepted as a certifiable educational discipline.

Core Curriculum:

I. B.A. (Liberal Arts):

A. *Required Courses:*

Course Title		Frequency of Offering	Hours
English 290:	Introduction to Film	every semester	3
English 390:	Film History I, Silents to 1945	one semester per year	3
English 391:	Film History II, 1945 to Present	one semester per year	3

B. *Either:*

Learning Resources 345: Basic Motion Picture Photography	every semester	3

and

Learning Resources 435: Motion Picture Production	one semester per year	3

or two of the following:

English 393: Film and Literature	one semester per year	3
English 490: Film Criticism	one semester per year	
Communication Arts and Sciences 426: Film and the Public Interest	alternate years	3

C. *Additional three hours from among:*

English 393, 490	(see above)	
Learning Resources 345, 435	(see above)	
Communication Arts and Sciences 426	(see above)	
Communication Arts and Sciences 326: Film and Television Documentary	alternate years	3
Political Science 301: Politics and the Cinema	one semester per year	3
	total hours required	18

II. B.A. (Teacher Education):

   A. *Required Courses:*
      English 290, 390, 391   (see above)
      Learning Resources 345, 435   (see above)

   B. *Two of the following:*
      English 393, 490   (see above)
      Communication Arts and Sciences 426   (see above)

   C. *One of the following:*
      Communication Arts and Sciences 326   (see above)
      Political Science 301   (see above)

                                 total hours required   24

Each semester different films are selected for the following courses; the following titles are typical.

English 290: Introduction to Film

    Introduction: film technique
        Lady from Shanghai, Orson Welles
    Documentary film
        Nanook of the North, Robert Flaherty
    Documentary and experimental film
        The Sixties, Charles Braverman
        Frank Film, Frank Mouris
        Woo Who? May Wilson, Amalie R. Rothschild
    Experimental film
        Un Chien Andalou, Luis Buñuel and Salvador Dali
        Meshes of the Afternoon, Maya Deren
        La Jetée, Chris Marker
    Genre film: westerns
        Stagecoach, John Ford
        The Man from Laramie, Anthony Mann
        Comanche Station, Budd Boetticher
    Genre film: musicals
        Swing Time, George Stevens
        The Gang's All Here, Busby Berkeley
        Meet Me in St. Louis, Vincente Minnelli
    Film authorship
        The Thirty-Nine Steps, Alfred Hitchcock
        Strangers on a Train, Alfred Hitchcock
    European film
        Play Time, Jacques Tati
        The Discreet Charm of the Bourgeoisie, Luis Buñuel
    Contemporary Hollywood film
        Harold and Maude, Hal Ashby

English 393: Film and Literature: Images of Women and Men in Film and Short Stories   An exploration of how men and women are presented in traditional and contemporary roles, including those of hero and heroine, wife, husband, and lover, father and mother, working or professional man or woman. Most of the short stories are in *Women and Men: Men and Women*, an anthology edited by William Smart (New York: St. Martin's Press, 1975).

Way Down East, D. W. Griffith; "The Old Chevalier," Isak Dinesen
Queen Christina, Rouben Mamoulian; "The Liberation," Jean Stafford
The Prisoner of Zenda, John Cromwell; "The Lady with the Dog," Anton Chekhov
Stagecoach, John Ford; "A Good Investment," Joyce Cary
Casablanca, Michael Curtiz; "Winter in July," Doris Lessing
Monkey Business, Howard Hawks; "Reservations: A Love Story," Peter Taylor
The Earrings of Madame de . . . ., Max Ophuls; "The White Stocking," D. H. Lawrence
Two Women, Vittorio de Sica; "The Five-forty-eight," John Cheever
Two for the Road, Stanley Donen; "Rope," Katherine Anne Porter
Chloe in the Afternoon, Eric Rohmer; "One off the Short List," Doris Lessing
Growing Up Female, Julia Reichert and Jim Klein; "Debut," Kristin Hunter
Joyce at 34, Joyce Chopra and Claudia Weill; "A Man and Two Women," Doris Lessing
Woo Who? May Wilson, Amalie R. Rothschild; *Right Out of History*, Johanna Demetrakis; "To Room 19," Doris Lessing
Kramer vs. Kramer, Robert Benton; "I Stand Here Ironing," Tillie Olson

Political Science 201: Politics and the Cinema   General topics include government, national and international political processes, and war. Robert Penn Warren's *All the King's Men* (New York: Bantam, 1973) and Michael Wood's *America in the Movies* (New York: Dell, 1975) are assigned written texts.

Citizen Kane, Orson Welles; *Mr. Smith Goes to Washington*, Frank Capra; *All the King's Men*, Robert Rossen; *The Great Dictator*, Charles Chaplin; *Fail-Safe*, Sidney Lumet; *Sahara*, Zoltan Korda; *The Caine Mutiny*, Edward Dmytryk; *A Sense of Loss*, Marcel Ophuls; *The Best Man*, Franklin Schaffner; *The Last Hurrah*, John Ford; *Modern Times*, Charles Chaplin; *The Spy Who Came In from the Cold*, Martin Ritt; *On the Waterfront*, Elia Kazan; *The Discreet Charm of the Bourgeoisie*, Luis Buñuel.

Film Studies at Pitzer College, Claremont

Beverle Houston

Dept. responsible for the film program	Film Studies Field Group
Full-time faculty in the intercollegiate dept.	3
Enrollment policies	
maximum class enrollment (if applicable)	15 per course in filmmaking others open
minimum class enrollment	N/A
average class enrollment	35 in history/criticism courses
Staffing	
% of film courses taught by part-time faculty	33%
% taught by full-time instructors or lecturers	0%
% taught by asst., assoc., and full-time professors	67%
Program size	
# of students enrolled in the film program in fall of 1981	120 (15 majors)
# of courses offered in the fall term of 1981	5
# of courses at all levels offered in the program	9
# of students enrolled at the institution	700

The unique characteristic of film studies at Pitzer College, Claremont, California (and at Claremont McKenna College, where the major is also available), is that the program is entirely interdisciplinary as well as intercollegiate. The student may concentrate in film, leading to a cross-disciplinary B.A. in film and fine arts, film and social sciences, film and liberal arts, or film and communication.

The Interdisciplinary and Intercollegiate Program

Pitzer College is a member of the Claremont colleges; the other undergraduate members of the cluster, each with its own curricular emphasis, are Pomona (liberal arts), Scripps (fine arts), Claremont McKenna College (formerly Claremont Men's—business and economics), and Harvey Mudd (science and engineering). Pitzer, with a student population of about seven hundred, emphasizes the social and behavioral sciences. An M.A. in literature and film is also available at the Claremont Graduate School.

The Claremont system as a whole has built into its structure the double emphasis of concentration and range. Each student is registered in a home college, where most of the course work, especially for the major, will be taken. After the freshman year, however, the student is free to cross-register in any of the other colleges. Thus in the normal course of things, the Claremont student becomes accustomed to a variety of curricular and disciplinary focuses as well as different pedagogical approaches.

There are no real departments at Pitzer; the faculty is organized into field groups, which sometimes follow the traditional disciplines but often do not, as in environmental studies, for example, which draws members from art, political studies, human ecology, anthropology, and other fields. Historically, as is often true in small colleges, there was no formal analysis of the question, From what extant fields will the study of film originate? Rather, film studies, like almost all other new majors at Claremont, came into existence through the advocacy of a group of interested faculty, in this case from English, art, and religion. At present, film studies draws its Pitzer College members from art, English, and sociology.

Like a number of other majors at Pitzer—mathematics and classics, for instance—film studies is intercollegiate as well, drawing on faculty and film courses from Pitzer (a search is planned for the near future), Claremont McKenna (Michael Riley), and from the School of Theology at Claremont, which is curator of the Flaherty estate and offers courses in communication and media, with special emphasis on the nonfiction film (Jack Coogan). In addition, Pomona and Scripps occasionally offer courses that are appropriate for film studies.

The three schools officially cooperating in the major—Pitzer, CMC, and the School of Theology—own a number of films basic to the study of the medium and have some access to the UCLA film archive and to various private, institutional, and commercial film collections as well as the usual rental resources. We often cooperate in bringing speakers and films to Claremont and run series or courses such as the recent one on silent film taught by David Shephard at the School of Theology. In addition, the various colleges also offer student-run film series.

The Approach to Film Study

The concentration in film studies approaches film as representation, as art, history, and ideology, accessible through the aesthetic, semiotic, and psycholanalytic procedures of textual analysis and through historical, sociological, and anthropological study of the means of production and effects of communication through media. Thus we emphasize the study of film texts, movements, and social implications rather than the making of films.

Of the required introductory course (taught each year by the film instructor at Pitzer or Mike Riley at CMC) we expect far too much. We try to introduce the concepts I've alluded to, mainly by asking, over and over in different forms, these questions: What are the different functions of film seen from various perspectives? What is the film for the people who make it—the writer, director, producer, star, technicians? What is it for those who view it and make meaning and money with it—the audiences who pay for it, the critics and scholars who reflect on it, the institutions that teach it? We hope to release the student from the unexamined belief that the realistic feature film is a "natural" phenomenon and to indicate instead what forces and networks converge to constitute the various kinds of filmmaking and film-viewing practices.

But students do not come to undergraduate film study courses with much background in the concepts and art forms that lie behind these ideas. We have to spend considerable time on the basics of art history, philosophy, psychology, criticism, and always on verbal (rather than cinematic) literacy. Thus our presentation of film-specific material is always partial in comparison to our goals. We are always searching for texts that reflect in a realistic way the wide-ranging goals of such an introductory course, fragmented under the pressure of a great deal of material in too little time and presented to students not accustomed to thinking in a conceptual framework, especially one that is, of necessity, constantly shifting. We often use Monaco's *How to Read a Film*, Knight's *The Liveliest Art*, and Stephenson and Debrix's *Film as Art*, but we change texts and rely on a large number of individual essays, particularly for theoretical and ideological material.

The introductory course is structured in a combination of historical-national categories of film (e.g., Russian montage, German expressionism, Italian neorealism) together with conceptual or ideological categories like "Cinematic and Cultural Codes," "The Avant-Garde, Abstract, or 'Underground' Film," or "Feminism and the Specular Problem: Who Looks at Whom in the Movies?" For example, we use the films of Griffith and of Hollywood in the thirties to examine the basic codes of narrative construction through editing and those of seamless continuity created through camerawork, lighting, and editing. We link these deconstructions to such concepts as the dream of the unified text and the positioning of the privileged viewer within the theater and within the text. In considering the specular problem, we offer von Sternberg's *Scarlet Empress* and Chick Strand's *Soft Fiction* as a contrasting pair of films demonstrating the conventions of identification and the controlling gaze and alternative ways of looking at the woman.

Other courses taken later are based on national cinemas, genres, thematic connections, directors, movements, or special topics, such as "Film and Politics" or "Women and Film."

Filmmaking

We believe that in order to understand the demands, possibilities, costs, joys, intransigencies, and articulations of the medium whose products are being held up to scrutiny, the student must have some hands-on experience of its apparatus and materials. Thus the undergraduate in all tracks of the major must take at least one course in Super-8 filmmaking and is offered the opportunity to take additional courses in Super-8 and 16mm for independent study. In 1980, we rebuilt an unused space into a well-set-up editing lab, classroom, and photo labs. We have an adequate amount of Super-8 visual, sound, and editing equipment for our present enrollments in filmmaking, which we hold to about thirty students each year. We have a very small amount of 16mm equipment and can sometimes arrange access to more. In addition, Pitzer has a small television studio, and the student may get some beginning experience in this medium as well, with further emphasis on tv in the film-communication track.

The student primarily interested in making films must be counseled about other schools with greater emphasis in this area, but the student who chooses to stay at Pitzer and work in this direction may choose the film and fine arts track, which requires a number of courses and independent studies in filmmaking, including the beginnings of animation and special effects (usually available through the art department at Scripps) as well as work in related fields, such as acting and directing (available through the intercollegiate drama progam) and in drawing and graphics (through the art departments at Pitzer and the other colleges). The student interested in ethnographic film may satisfy certain requirements in anthropology through visual work.

We do not conceive of ourselves as offering a full program in filmmaking, locating our strengths instead in the historical-analytical work of the liberal arts and social sciences, as influenced by the interventions of recent theorizing in film study. For the student who has that special obsession with making films, we argue the value of a diversified, analytic undergraduate education, and we recommend that he or she move on to graduate work at the several universities offering rich programs in production.

Specifics of the Program

For each track of the film studies concentration, the student must take about six courses specifically in film (including the introduction and basic filmmaking— "The Grammar of Film") as well as an additional six or seven courses in the related disciplines of the chosen track. For example, the student choosing the film and social sciences track might take "History and Aesthetics of Film, an Introduction," "American Genres," "Film and Politics: Special Topics," "Central Women in Novel and Film," "The Non-Fiction Film," "The Films of Orson Welles," "Experimental Film and Video," "The Grammar of Film." In related disciplines, he or she might take two anthropology courses with a visual or communications emphasis, a course in "The Sociology of Media," and three psychology courses involving, say, perception and cognition, communication, or small-group processes.

The Future

As a new program, we are still developing our resources. All courses are not available each year; thus the richness of the program may vary for individual students. Above all, we need more courses, some of which we foster by cultivating our colleagues' interests in film and related subjects till they flower into new courses in our flexible curriculum. We also bring in filmmakers and scholars to teach one course from time to time. In 1980–81, for example, Gene Youngblood taught an analytic course in experimental video. Our long-range plans (hopes) involve developing richer faculty resources in filmmaking as well as in history and criticism, but we must face the fact that these are not expanding times.

The Four-Track Interdisciplinary Film Studies Major
Students concentrating in film must choose one of the four interdisciplinary tracks described below. Each track requires a minimum of twelve courses, six in film and six in a related discipline. The requirements presented below are offered as a minimum and are aimed at providing a reasonable interdisciplinary distribution of courses. To complete the concentration in each track, students are expected to work closely with advisers in choosing courses that will develop individual interests and goals; advisers must approve each course that is to be counted in the concentration.

All film concentrators are required to take:

Pitzer Film 107: History and Aesthetics of Film, an Introduction *or*
CMC English 121: Film: An Introduction *and*
Pitzer Film 182: The Grammar of Film (introduction to 8mm filmmaking).

1. The Film and Fine Arts Track

Advanced Filmmaking
Scripps 123: Film Arts
At least two other film courses
A course in design, drawing, or photography
A twentieth-century art history course
A course in either directing or acting
At least three other courses in creative writing, theater arts, arts, dance, music, or photography

2. The Film and Social Sciences Track

Anthropological Film (when available)
A documentary film course
A course focusing on film and society, such as Women and Film (Pitzer) or Politics and Film (CMC)
At least one other film course
Six courses from the following disciplines, including one in each of three fields: sociology, anthropology, psychology, political studies

3. The Film and Humanities Track

CMC English 124: Film and the Novel
STC Theater 271: History of the Theatrical Film
At least two other film courses
A course in the history of Western civilization or two other history courses
Two literature courses
One art history course
At least two other humanities courses
Film and humanities concentrators will also be expected to demonstrate a reading and conversational competence in at least one foreign language. At Pitzer, this will mean four courses (including one in conversation) or the equivalent.

4. The Film and Communications Track

At least three other film courses
One tv course (production or writing)
Two or three courses in sociology or psychology that focus on communication
    or intergroup relations, including Sociology of Communications (Pitzer)
Two or three additional communications-related courses (such as Mass Culture,
    Perception and Cognition, Small Group Processes)

Students interested in film production are strongly urged to take Introductory Accounting or Microeconomics. Students in all tracks who plan to continue in film studies are strongly urged to become competent in a foreign language.

Film-Related Courses Often Recommended for the
Interdisciplinary Film Studies Tracks

Social Psychology
Small Group Processes
Psychology of Creative Behavior
Group Dynamics
Perception and Cognition
Human Communication and Critical Thinking
Sociology of Communications
Acting
Directing
Film Arts (introduction to animation and techniques of personal filmmaking)
Drawing
Language and Culture
Animal Communication and Human Language
Classical Mythology
Music in Culture
Modern American History
Economics or Economic History

Film Studies at Occidental College

Marsha Kinder* and Chick Strand

Dept. responsible for the film program   Department of Theater Arts and Rhetoric
and Department of English

Full-time faculty in the dept.	1½
Enrollment policies	
maximum class enrollment (if applicable)	N/A
minimum class enrollment	N/A
average class enrollment	35
Staffing	
% of film courses taught by part-time faculty	20%
% taught by full-time instructors or lecturers	0%
% taught by asst., assoc., and full professors	80%
Program size	
# of students enrolled in the film program in fall of 1981	50
# of courses offered in the fall term of 1981	4
# of courses at all levels offered in the program	12
# of students enrolled at the institution	1,700

Occidental College is a high-quality, small liberal arts college located in Los Angeles, with 1,700 undergraduates and 120 full-time faculty. Consistent with the diversity and flexibility of Occidental's curriculum, the college offers several alternatives in film studies, all of which emphasize an interdisciplinary approach.

The focus is on independent, personal filmmaking and, more specifically, on avant-garde and documentary film. Most of our courses emphasize film production rather than film history, analysis, or criticism; however, the production courses do cover these other aspects. For instance, the beginning film production course includes the showing and discussion of avant-garde work from Méliès to Brakhage. The students are given cameras the first day and begin to make their own films immediately. Our philosophy is directed to a hands-on approach, to the development of individual style and direction independent of established film theory; it stresses the creative process rather than the academic and intellectual analysis of film art. Many of our courses are on documentaries and films of the third world. Because of the interdisciplinary nature of our program, many of the students are involved in political, social, or ethnographic directions in film.

Most schools have neglected documentary film and film as an art form in favor of the narrative entertainment film viewed as artifact in order to justify film study in an academic atmosphere. We see no problem in the idea that creative excellence is as valid as academic excellence or that creating powerful and meaningful images can be accepted as an academic pursuit. Therefore we have combined studio art (film/video production) with the more traditional intellectual study of film as work of art. We are not convinced that the making of art should be considered a purely intellectual enterprise or that the liberal arts should stop short of offering the opportunity for artistic pursuit. We believe that knowing how to make a film is as important as learning to be an intelligent and aware viewer. We are much less interested in developing standards than we are in developing the individual student in his or her own terms.

Two members of the staff currently teach film—critic and scholar David James, and filmmaker Chick Strand. The film and video production faculty person is a well-known artist and the theory, history, and criticism faculty person is a professional film journalist. In terms of the requirements for faculty, we seek professionals who are both teachers and recognized working artists and writers in their own fields.

Each program combines an emphasis on film within a social and political framework with an opportunity to use film as a medium of personal artistic expression. Despite our very restrictive budget for film studies, we are able to offer our students a choice among the following four programs.

1. *An Independent Pattern of Study in Film or Media Studies.*   An independent major must be declared by the beginning of the junior year. The pattern of courses (at least eight) can be tailored to suit the particular interests of the individual student and must be arranged in consultation with three members of the faculty, who function as an advisory committee that approves the course of study and designs and administers a comprehensive examination. Some past topics have been "Budgeting for Feature Films," "Ocean on Film," and "Animation."

2. *A Major in Theater Arts and Rhetoric with an Emphasis on Film.*   All students are required to take "Creative Film I," "Creative Film II," "Creative Video I," "Creative Video II," "Aesthetics of the Cinema," "Creative Film III," and "Anthropology 10." In addition they must take three of the following courses: "Basic

Photographic Communications," "Third World Films," "Creative Writing for the Screen," "Studies in Documentary and Ethnographic Films," "Documentary Film Workshop," and "Literature and Film."

3. A Comparative Literature Major with an Emphasis on Film. This major requires a core of four world literature survey courses, a methodology course, plus six courses in film studies.

4. An English Major with an Emphasis on Film. This major requires ten courses in English plus four courses in film, including "Literature and Film."

Despite our small staff, we have increased the number of courses and curricular flexibility within film studies in the following ways:

1. Independent Study. Besides their regular course load, each of the three staff members in film studies also supervises individual students on individual projects, for which the student receives full academic credit. This might include the making of a film, videotape, screenplay, or research project. This option is particularly helpful to advanced students.

2. Adjuncts. Every year a number of adjunct faculty are hired to teach courses in a variety of departments. Sometimes this results in additional courses in film studies. For example, in 1980–81 the economics department offered "Economics of Mass Communication Industries" and American studies presented "Chicano Studies," taught by a leading Chicano filmmaker, Jesus Trevino (*Yo Soy Chicano* and *Raices de Sangre*).

3. Special Summer Programs. Five courses are regularly taught in summer school in photography and film: "Beginning Film Production," "Advanced Film Production," "Creative Writing for the Screen," "Beginning Photography," and "Advanced Photography." These five courses are currently being taught as workshops by Chick Strand in San Miguel de Allende, Mexico. In addition, several combined courses have been taught. For example, David Buge from the anthropology department, whose field is archaeology, and Chick Strand taught a combined course in film and archaeology on a working field trip to Santa Fe, New Mexico. Students interested in archaeology worked in the dig, while students of film made a documentary film about it. The result was an interesting film about the methodology of archaeology as well as the various cultural and psychological factors involved in working on scientific research within an isolated environment. The film was shown by CBS on one of its public service programs.

Through our study abroad programs during the summer, many students have taken advantage of independent studies courses to document various aspects of their educational experiences, editing their footage when they returned to campus. In several cases, an outstanding film has resulted.

4. Work Study Programs. Many students are able to broaden their film experience by either working through the Federal Work Study Program on campus in a technical capacity or by gaining experience in film programming, directing festivals and shows. In addition, students who work in a program off campus in various film capacities are also able to work out an independent course in which their off-campus work experiences can count for course credit.

5. Internships. Supervised internships are available to students at film journals, such as *Film Quarterly*, *Quarterly Review of Film Studies*, and *Dreamworks*, in broadcasting, and in advertising. Internships are also available with film-production companies, screenwriting agencies, and experimental film theaters. Because of the location of the college, students can also be exposed to the in-house apprenticeships and programs offered by the commercial film industry.

6. Alternation of Courses.   The full-time teaching load is two courses per term. Since Occidental's academic year is divided into three ten-week terms (plus two five-week summer sessions), each full-time faculty member teaches six courses per year. To increase the number of film courses she can offer, Chick Strand teaches several of her courses every other year.

7. General Course Titles with Shifting Emphasis.   David James uses a different strategy to increase curricular flexibility. Although he offers the same three courses every year, each term they shift their focus and students are allowed to take them for credit more than once.

Description of Courses

Theater Arts and Rhetoric 55: Basic Film Production (Strand)   This course introduces students to the idea of using film as an art form, exposes them to the work of artists in the field, and guides them through their first experience in making a film. During the course of the ten weeks, students are shown approximately forty experimental films. During the first two weeks, we take a historical approach and see works by Cocteau, Buñuel, Clair, and the early abstractionists. Later we see works of more contemporary artists—e.g., Brakhage, Baillie, Snow, Nelson, Conner, Frampton. Films are discussed less from a critical viewpoint than from the artists' viewpoints, in an attempt to understand the creative process involved. For most students, this is their first exposure to film as an art form. In fact, most students have no idea that it is possible that film can be a medium for personal poetic expression.

Students are required to write an in-depth journal that includes dreams, ideas, personal philosophy, experiences both physical and spiritual, ideas and conclusions concerning world events, and personal events, past and present. They are asked to relate the things in the journal to their feelings about art and their involvement in it as well as to their objective analysis of and subjective feelings about the films they see in class. They are required to make a Super-8 film, with sound (explained below). No restrictions are made as to content, direction, subject, or kind of film made. Students are encouraged to make any film they wish. This course does not include much technical data beyond enough training in the use of the camera and simple editing technology to let students put a film together. Thus the students have few preconceived notions about filmmaking and, for this first experience, are left totally free to explore the medium in their own terms.

Theater Arts and Rhetoric 137: Advanced Film Seminar (Strand)   This course can be considered a continuation of the beginning course. Students are again shown experimental films, although fewer and longer ones, with a greater variety of approach to what is considered "experimental." Students do not write a journal for the course; the sole requirement is to make a film. They are given much more technical information and at this point are introduced to synchronous sound. The class is much smaller, and individual film projects are discussed at length. The students learn the technology by doing. Although each student makes his or her own film, the entire class is involved in the making of one other film. Each student is required to crew on this film and takes on each job (filming in sync, assembling dailies, recording sound, making editing decisions, laying tracks, mixing, cutting negative, A and B rolling, and dealing with the lab) in order to learn the technology. Again, no restrictions are placed on individual film work; however, the student is encouraged to make a synchronous sound film (not necessarily lip-sync). In addition, each student has one day in which the entire class is at his or her disposal for crew or help in this film. The entire class goes on location with the student, who may choose to send members of the class off or utilize them in one capacity or another during the filming day. What is important here is that the student must discover independently his or her own creative process and relate it to the kind of film that is evolving. Students interested in narrative film can proceed in a semiprofessional manner and use the facilities at hand. Students may also choose to work alone. By the end of the course, all of the students will have experienced a variety of approaches and possibilities in filmmaking. No student feels pressured to make one kind of film or another, and the student who does not seem to be finding a direction is exposed to many alternatives.

Theater Arts and Rhetoric 81: Creative Writing for the Screen (Strand) Students must submit a sample of their writing and obtain the permission of the instructor in order to register. Class is limited to twelve students. Students are required to complete many writing assignments, and the final project is a screenplay. The first assignment is to write a suspense scene with dialogue. Then the students are asked to write a monologue, and then a scene between two characters, which they must direct on videotape. The class discusses these projects, giving suggestions as to how to make the scenes "play." After the students start to get a feeling about how to write language that will be spoken and acted, the process of acting out their scenes tapers off. They begin writing more and reading aloud less.

Part of the course is then directed to the editing of dialogue from documentary sources. The students are asked to get an interview on tape and then to edit and rearrange the transcript of the interview until it becomes simple, to the point, and as powerful as possible. For many of those who find it very difficult to "make up" situations, this becomes a way to discover hidden creative writing capabilities. For the students who find it easier to tap their imaginative resources, this assignment enables them to see more clearly a way to develop character and relationships. Coupled with the next assignment—the writing of an outline for a possible documentary film dealing with the interview subject—this approach also helps them to draw upon real situations in order to build up action, drama, and suspense. The final script can be narrative, documentary, or experimental. Students who wish to write a narrative film must do so in a standardized commercial form. Those who wish to write a documentary must do so based upon information they have gathered in the field. Those who wish to write an experimental film are free to use whatever form they evolve for their own particular project. Although this form may consist of notes, drawings, or statements describing cinematic visions, it must be accompanied by a paper stating their artistic concerns (which could possibly range from how the writings of André Breton have influenced their thinking about the project to their passion for looking at the arrangement of the items in friends' refrigerators).

Theater Arts and Rhetoric 32: Third World Films (Strand) Students are shown feature films made in the third world by third world directors as well as some films made about third world cultures by Western filmmakers. Some of the films shown are *Memories of Underdevelopment, Harvest, Green Wall, Pather Panchali, Calcutta,* and *Cool World.* Students are required to keep an intensive journal that comments on their experiences with and feelings about third world people and how their feelings have changed during the course. They are also required to do research on the topics covered in their journals and to spend what would ordinarily be study time (twelve hours per week, or three hours for every hour spent in class) as a volunteer worker in any capacity with any agency dealing with the poor or with disadvantaged people who identify primarily with a culture other than the dominant American one. In short, this work enables them to deal with people who are not ordinarily a part of the students' own immediate cultural environment. The term "third world" is broadened here to include a variety of possibilities: for example, one student worked with prisoners; another on a hot line for rape victims; another student, who is gay, worked with straight men who had drinking problems. The student keeps another journal covering volunteer work experiences or may combine the two journals. Films seen in class are discussed in terms of the cultures involved and are related to the students' new experiences in their volunteer work. The final project is a film or videotape about the people they have been working with. Although this course may seem to deal more with personal development than with filmmaking, it is this growth that prepares the film artist to see the world outside in a more objective way and to transform it into creative material for subjective film work with greater clarity, power, and openness.

Theater Arts and Rhetoric 135: Ethnographic Documentary Films (Strand)   This course includes the history of documentary filmmaking from *Nanook of the North* to *Gray Gardens*. Analysis of the difference between the ethnographic and the documentary approach is presented, along with theory on propagandistic, persuasive, poetic, argumentative, and descriptive approaches. Students are required to make a documentary film.

Theater Arts and Rhetoric 136: Documentary Film Workshop (Strand)   This is a course for advanced students who already know how to use the sync-sound equipment. Class enrollment is small and is divided into three or four groups, consisting of four students each. Each student is required to present a proposal for a documentary film. Each group then chooses one of the proposals and makes the film. Each group is given a budget, and the students in each group must make all film decisions together. The entire class only meets a few times during the quarter to share problems and experiences, exchange ideas, show rushes, and discuss progress. Each group works as a unit and meets with the professor for help and guidance. Some of the group projects have documented a punk rock band, a radio station in Santa Barbara, and a portrait of a black street artist. In the workshop course, the students gain the experience of working in crews, cooperating on a film, and working as much away from the academic atmosphere as possible. In this way, they see what it is like to make a film on the "outside." Each individual student is required to keep a journal consisting of personal experiences, development of film skills, and new insights acquired on the group project.

Theater Arts and Rhetoric 31: Basic Photographic Communications (Strand)   Students are taught how to use their 35mm cameras, to develop black-and-white film, and to make and mount prints. The class goes on six or seven field trips for shoots. Experimentation in the darkroom is taught and encouraged. Very few assignments are required: the student must turn in five prints with definite subjects (light and shadow, a portrait, human interest, nature, documentary) along with a portfolio of at least twenty mounted prints and a special project that can range from experimentation with techniques to a focus on subject matter. Again the emphasis is on personal artistic development rather than exercises. Students are shown film portraits of photographic artists such as Weston, Cunningham, and Gordon Parks; slides of photographs, which range from photojournalism to fashion photography; portraiture and the works of such artists as Mathew Brady, Arthur Penn, Bullock, Ullsman, and Duane Michaels. Students are not expected to know the work of individual artists but instead are taught how to begin looking at photographs with an eye to reevaluating the way they make their own photographs.

Theater Arts and Rhetoric 131: Advanced Photography (Strand)   Students are encouraged to begin developing their own perspectives and to explore new directions, discovering their own style. Many visiting artists come to the class to show and discuss their work and their creative processes. Students are required to turn in a portfolio of work.

Freshman Seminar   Occidental has a program in which each department teaches writing skills to freshmen in the context of special fields. In film, a freshman writing seminar has been taught with the following themes: cinema, human alienation, and cinema, the human condition. Although the main focus of the course is to help freshmen students develop good writing skills, students are also exposed to various means of cinematic expression and, perhaps more important, to recent history. Films shown include *Triumph of the Will*, *Night and Fog*, *Hearts and Minds*, and *Gimme Shelter*.

Equipment and Facilities

Film equipment at Occidental is all in Super-8. We have purchased a complete Super-8 sound facility (the Cambridge System developed by Ricky Leacock) so that students can make complete and professional Super-8 sound films in lip sync. Although some students have managed on their own to make lip-sync films in 16mm, Occidental does not have 16mm facilities. With the Cambridge double system, students can learn professional film techniques with the least cost to them and without an enormous capital investment by the college. Students can be technically prepared for graduate work in the film schools and for professional work in the commercial field. For beginning students we have a number of Super-8 cameras, editors, and projectors (one set for each four students) and a sound system consisting of a multisync tape deck, amp, turntable, stereo tape deck, cassette recorder, mixer, and speakers. Although the beginners do not have sync sound available to them, they can still choose to have a fairly complicated sound track on their films. If they wish, they can have four tracks in sync with each other, though not in exact sync with the projector.

Creative Video I (Strand)   Video is studied as an art form with emphasis on basic production skills. The medium is explored as a tool for creative and educational self-confrontation and communication. The course includes an overview of television and art in the twentieth century, and video is seen as the alternative to standard television and "standard art" practices.

Besides examining current applications of video through the screening of artists' tapes, guest lectures, and field trips to various creative centers, students are expected to produce projects such as off-the-air news transformations, a video diary, and a final personal video essay exploring the idiosyncrasies of the medium. The work is done in ½" reel to reel, VHS, or ¾" cassette, when available.

Creative Video II (Strand)   A continuation and solidification of the basic video principles discovered during the first course. The emphasis now is on directing, lighting, editing, image and sound processing, and the goal of the course is the completion of a complex video piece. Besides producing their individual work, students are expected to collaborate on other students' projects to learn more about the different aspects of video production. If available, the format used is ¾" cassette.

Theater Arts and Rhetoric 56: The Aesthetics of Cinema (James)   This course is required of all theater arts and rhetoric majors (regardless of emphasis) and of all English teaching majors. Thus although the films change each year, there are many constants:

- an introduction to the main lines of international film history;
- an introduction to critical theory, including realist and formalist aesthetics, auteur and genre approaches, and the application of Marxist and feminist ideology, phenomenology, depth psychology, and semiotics to film criticism;
- an emphasis on practical film criticism;
- a personal journal documenting the individual student's film-viewing experiences in the course;
- a term project—a film, screenplay, or critical essay.
- Films are screened on Monday, discussed on Tuesday and Wednesday, and then screened again on Thursday. In this way students are better able to perceive their own growth in their ability to see, understand, and appreciate each film.

English 30: Literature and Film (James)   Although this course changes its content every year, it always includes the following:

- a comparison between both media, stressing the unique resources of each;
- an examination of adaptation theory;
- a comparison between literary and film criticism;
- the opportunity for students to write at least two critical essays;
- the opportunity for students to adapt a story or play to a screenplay, film, or video project.

For example, "Shakespeare on Film" was taught in collaboration with two other classes the same term in acting and Shakespeare so that students could see the same films and performances and collaborate on term projects. Some of the film students, for instance, did videotapes using the acting performances of students in the acting class. Other courses included "Ingmar Bergman," "America in the Sixties through Literature and Film," "The Gothic Novel and the Horror Film," and "Literary Film Analogies." The latter course included not only direct adaptations of novels, stories, and plays but also works that involved more than two media and raised theoretical issues of adaptations, for example, Cammel and Roeg's *Performance* as an adaptation of Borges' story "The South" and Hesse's novel *Steppenwolf*; Godard's *Contempt* as a self-reflexive adaptation of both Moravia's novel *A Ghost at Noon* and Homer's epic *The Odyssey*; and Herzog's *Kaspar Hauser* as an alternative to Handke's play *Kaspar* and Wassermann's novel *Caspar Hauser*.

In "The Gothic Novel and the Horror Film," a course focused on genre, students had to adapt two scenes from either *The Shining* or *Interview with the Vampire*, works that were being made into films but had not yet been released. Such an assignment has interesting pedagogical implications because it ensures that the critical evaluation of the work will extend far beyond the temporal limits of the term. Students learn to see in film classes, and this marked improvement is experienced daily outside the classroom.

American Studies 50: Comparative Studies in Literature, Film, and Culture   This course changes its content every year but always focuses primarily on American film within a broader social and political context. Recent examples are "Sex Roles in American Literature," "Film and Society," "The Myth of the American Hero in the Life and Works of Orson Welles," and "Film Studies in General Education Courses."

In addition to these courses in film studies, Occidental also offers film as part of the form and substance of its general education courses, which are required of all students and are at the center of the liberal arts curriculum. Both James and Strand lecture on film within this program. Here are some examples of how specific films have been used in these interdisciplinary courses in 1979–80.

European Culture (taken by all freshmen)   This course opened with a screening of *2001: A Space Odyssey* and the reading of Homer's *Odyssey*. The opening lecture by Marsha Kinder discussed the film in terms of its synchronic and diachronic approaches to human progress, with special attention to the role of technology as an extension of the human body and to the persistence of the unknown. The two-course sequence in European culture was organized around the alternation between certain synchronic themes or bipolarities (e.g., the self and other, the individual and society) and the diachronic (tracing of certain cultural components through history). By opening this historical course with a film from the sixties, we were challenging the diachronic organization both in form and in content. The first term ended with the reading of Shakespeare's *King Lear* and the viewing of film adaptations by the British director Peter Brook and the Soviet filmmaker Grigori Kozintsev, offering two quite different interpretations filtered through different cultural perspectives. In the second term of the course, which went through the nineteenth century, film continued to be used to stress the synchronic perspective. For example, after reading Defoe's *Robinson Crusoe*, the students saw, discussed, and heard a lecture about Nicolas Roeg's *Walkabout*, a contemporary film that exposes the racist and imperialist assumptions of the eighteenth-century classic and helps to account for the survival power of the Robinson Crusoe myth.

American Culture 1: Contemporary American Culture (taken by all sophomores)   Since this course focuses on American culture since World War I, film plays a more central role than in the "European Culture" course. Both readings and films were assigned every week. The course opened with Charlie Chaplin's *Modern Times*, which introduced the three major emphases of the course: the roles of economics, technology, and media in twentieth-century America. In the week in which we read Galbraith on the stock market crash and the depression, we saw *The Grapes of Wrath* and "The Lullaby of Broadway" dance number from a 1930s Busby Berkeley musical, providing two contrasting ways in which the art of that period was confronting or disguising the national economic disaster. *Citizen Kane* and the career of Orson Welles were used as a means of examining the rise to power of the mass media in America—the newspaper, the radio, and the movies, all of which were compared with the later development of television. In the week devoted to sexual politics, we saw and discussed the documentaries *Harlan County, U.S.A.* and *Woman to Woman*—both directed by women and both stressing the need for sexual, racial, and economic coalitions among the oppressed. By using so many films in a great variety of ways in a course that was not defined as part of film studies, the interdisciplinary staff of the American culture faculty (including historians, anthropologists, psychologists, economists, literary critics, and art historians) was reaffirming an assumption that is basic to the curriculum at Occidental—that a knowledge of film, both as a significant contemporary art form and as a medium of mass communication, is essential to a liberal arts education.

Note

*Marsha Kinder is now on the faculty of the University of Southern California.

Film Studies at the University of Illinois at Urbana-Champaign

Robert L. Carringer

Dept. responsible for the film program	See text
Full-time faculty in the dept.	6
Enrollment policies	
maximum class enrollment (if applicable)	35 per section
minimum class enrollment	varies with level of instruction
average class enrollment	30 per section
Staffing	
% of film courses taught by part-time faculty	25%
% taught by full-time instructors or lecturers	10%
% taught by asst., assoc., and full professors	65%
Program size	
# of students enrolled in the film program in fall of 1982	950 students enrolled in film courses (18 concentrators in the program)
# of courses offered in the fall term of 1982	15
# of courses offered in all levels offered in the program	28
# of students enrolled at the institution	34,914

At the University of Illinois at Urbana-Champaign, the critical, aesthetic, and historical study of film is the province of the School of Humanities in the College of Liberal Arts and Sciences. (Filmmaking, on the other hand, is taught in the School of Art and Design in the College of Fine and Applied Arts.) The departmental entity in the School of Humanities is the Unit for Cinema Studies, which is charged not only with offering its own courses and hiring faculty but also with coordinating interdisciplinary course offerings in film in nine different humanities departments and with setting and maintaining policies and standards in all academic cinema studies matters on the campus. At the undergraduate level the Unit for Cinema Studies administers a concentration (major) in cinema studies and, jointly with the College of Education, a teacher-education minor in cinema studies. Although there is no advanced degree in cinema studies per se at Illinois, there are opportunities in several humanities departments (English, French, comparative literature, history, speech communication) for students to devise programs with film concentrations and write Ph.D. theses on film topics, and the unit assists these students by making films and other resources and facilities (such as a Steenbeck viewing table) available for their research.

Who should have the privilege and responsibility of teaching film? According to one view, the professionals—those with academic training or other formal accreditation in the field, such as publication—should band together in their own department and define the standards and boundaries of the discipline. According to another view, the study of film flourishes best where a multiplicity of historical, cultural, and other perspectives is encouraged, and the proper institutional arrangement is a loose confederation of faculty associated with a variety of background disciplines. Either approach has its own special virtues as well as drawbacks. While the film department arrangement tends to foster more rigorous critical standards, it also encourages parochialism and overspecialization. And while the film center arrangement encourages breadth and versatility, it also makes the application of consistent standards difficult and frequently leads to curricular chaos. An attempt has been made in the program at Illinois to preserve the best features of each model. There are two categories of courses in the undergraduate concentration, "core courses" and "interdisciplinary courses." With one exception, the core courses are administered by the Unit for Cinema Studies and taught by faculty with formal appointments in cinema studies. (The exception is "Introduction to Film," which is housed in English for institutional reasons but is internationalist in content and staffed by assistants from several departments.) Eighteen hours of core courses are required in the concentration—the introduction to film, a two-semester world film survey, a course in film theory and criticism, and six hours of individually directed research. The interdisciplinary courses, on the other hand, are taught in a variety of humanities departments, such as French, English, and history. These treat film as a historical phenomenon, and they employ a variety of social, cultural, and literary perspectives. Film concentrators are required to complete eighteen hours of these interdisciplinary courses.

Though there have been film courses in the humanities at Illinois since the 1950s, film as a large-scale academic enterprise was a product of the 1970s. In the late 1960s, seventy-five students per semester were enrolled in cinema studies courses. By the fall of 1972, student requests for film courses had risen to more than seven hundred per semester. By 1975 it had risen to more than nine hundred. Instead of peaking at this point (as might be expected), student demand continued its steady rise throughout the second half of the 1970s, and the current rate is nearly 1,500 student requests for film courses per semester. Like many other institutions, the University of Illinois was insufficiently prepared for the mushrooming of enrollments in film, and the early 1970s were sometimes chaotic. In a time of dramatic enrollment declines in the humanities generally, there was suddenly an apparently endless clientele for film courses, and at some institutions probably more than one faculty job was saved by hastily prepared popular topics courses in film. In the mid-1970s, however, the University of Illinois took certain fundamental steps in an effort to ensure the academic integrity of the discipline and the program. A new course was created at the 100-level, "Introduction to Film." Teaching assignment to this course was made conditional on professional training or previous teaching experience in the field or, alternatively, completion of a semester-long professional seminar in the teaching of film. Most significantly, the decision was made to organize "Introduction to Film" not as a large lecture course but as an individual section course. The sections come together for the weekly film screening but meet individually in small lecture-discussion sessions of thirty students each. One criticism of this arrangement is that some students may receive their basic training exclusively from a teaching assistant rather than from full-time faculty, but it was felt that the opportunity for individual contact and extended discussion and analysis of the films outweighed the other consideration. (Roughly half of the sections are assigned to graduate teaching assistants, the other half to full-time faculty.) A lid was placed on enrollments in the "Introduction to Film" course to keep it manageable (eighteen sections of thirty students), and this has been maintained even though the course is currently ninety percent (or 468 student requests) overenrolled. "Introduction to Film" was made a prerequisite for entry into the 200- and 300- level courses, and other film teaching at the 100-level (especially of popular topics courses) was formally discouraged. In a typical semester, there will be roughly a dozen courses available at the 200- and 300-levels—the survey, the theory course, and one or more courses each in national cinemas (French, Slavic, Germanic), genres (comedy, musicals, horror), directors (Hitchcock, Bergman, Welles), and special topics (adaptation, production design, the coming of sound).

One of the most serious problems facing a film program is the difficulty of continuous access to the primary texts in the field. In the typical circumstance, a 16mm print is rented for one showing only and is returned to the distributor the day after the playdate. When the film is discussed in class under such an arrangement, it is not possible to resolve matters of interpretation by reference to the text. Sometimes a script or other kind of secondary material may be available, but in many cases a debatable point has to be left as simply a matter of one person's memory versus another's. Six weeks later students are asked to write intelligently on an exam about a film they have not had the opportunity to see again, much less subject to close scrutiny. Understandably, colleagues and administrators may have serious doubts about whether academic standards can be maintained in such circumstances. And the rental fees continue semester afer semester without any kind of equity or amortization features accruing to the institution. There are several partial remedies to the access problem. A fortunate few happen to be located near a major archive (University of Rochester) or maintain their own archive (UCLA) or have a faculty member who is also a film collector (New York University). Many distributors offer permanent leases on some of their films, at rates averaging more than $1,000 per film; while this is beyond the means of most individual institutions, several cooperative ventures among institutions (such as the C.I.C. Consortium among the Big Ten and the Shakespeare Film Co-op) have been successful. Several hundred feature films that are in the public domain can be purchased outright at prices averaging $350 to $400 for black and white. These are mainly silent titles, foreign classics of the thirties, forties, and fifties, and American sound features for which the copyright was never renewed. This is the route followed at Illinois. Ever since the program was first funded in the early seventies, the largest share of each budget has been allocated for the purchase of films. The result was that after a few years the rental budgets leveled off and in some cases actually dropped. At present most titles in the categories mentioned are available locally for classroom use, and rental budgets tend to be spent on a relatively small number of high-priced recent titles.

With the advent of ½" videotapes and videodiscs, there is increasing pressure to switch the acquisitions emphasis to these much less costly formats in spite of the serious technical limitations involved (the video image is a different size and shape from the film image, and the dynamic light range in video is considerably less than that of film). Dramatic improvements in the quality of video resolution are expected in the coming decade, particularly in the area of large-screen video projection. For instance, with new video projection capabilities being installed at Illinois in the summer of 1983 we will be able to increase horizontal resolution from select sources to 450–500 lines. Further developments in this area will be dealt with as they occur, but because of the problems of lighting and image size in video, for the immediate future the minimum standard for classroom projection at Illinois will continue to be the best available 16mm print.

Administrators already doling out scarce resources for film rentals and purchases do not like to be reminded of yet another of film's special and costly needs—that films should be projected under proper conditions and with the best equipment available. A totally dark lecture room in one of the sciences buildings, a single noisy projector run by the instructor or an assistant, and a break to change reels each time is probably a much more common situation than most of us imagine. Yet at most institutions resources tend to follow enrollments, and this situation should be exploited for the good of the discipline. At Illinois, for instance, a rigorous lobbying effort finally paid off a few years ago when the campus administration agreed to convert a lecture hall into a screening facility for film classes, with suitable blackout conditions, rheostat controls on the lights for notetaking, an enclosed projection booth, 35mm and 16mm projection in all screen formats, and capability for both ¾" and ½" videotape and laser-vision videodiscs. A projectionist was assigned to the facility for film class screenings from 1 to 10 p.m. Monday through Thursday and 1 to 5 on Friday. Projection service is also available for the individual classroom meetings, as well as Athena analytic projectors and portable videotape and videodisc playback units.

Perhaps the most elusive problem of all has been to get the films into the hands of the students themselves. If students are to be expected to write intelligently about films, they must have the means to subject them to critical scrutiny. Again, videotapes and videodiscs represent a partial solution. In response to this need, the University of Illinois Library in 1978 installed a media center with individual videotape playback units in the undergraduate library and provided the funds for a core collection of videotapes in the subject area of film. The center contains four playback units, each with capacity for four headphone sets so that students can view videotaped materials individually or in small groups. The holdings of the center are used as the basis of writing assignments, particularly in the introductory course. Typical assignments involve sequence analysis and comparative studies of directors and genres. Most instructors agree that there was a dramatic rise in the quality of student writing after the installation of the media center—an outcome that significantly outweighs the loss of image quality involved in using videotapes. A permanent acquisitions line to develop the videotape collection has been secured. The next step is expansion into videodiscs, which librarians regard as more suitable than videotapes for archival use.

A special feature of the program at Illinois is a teacher-education minor in cinema studies. This was devised in response to an increasing need for multi-qualified teachers at the secondary school level in the state of Illinois. The minor is intended to be combined with a concentration in a more traditional field, such as history, languages, or literature. The evidence indicates that persons in these areas of declining enrollment who have an additional specialization in a field like film sometimes have an edge in the job market.

As with many institutions, the impetus for creating the program at Illinois came from existing faculty with appointments in film-related disciplines. A top priority recently has been to bring in new faculty. In 1981–82, one new tenure-track position was created in the Unit for Cinema Studies (it was filled by a specialist in Japanese cinema from the Ph.D. program in cinema studies at the University of Southern California); a second tenure-track position has been created in English beginning in 1983–84 (a specialist in feminism and film theory from the Ph.D. program in rhetoric at Berkeley has been hired); and an additional position in art history is expected to be authorized in the near future.

Courses

Asterisks designate open-topics courses; sample topics of recent offerings are given in parentheses.

Core Courses

Introduction to Film (English 104)
Survey of World Cinema I: The Beginnings to 1930 (Humanities 261)
Survey of World Cinema II: 1930s to the Present (Humanities 262)
Film Theory and Criticism (Humanities 361)
*Undergraduate Seminar (Sound and Image) (Humanities 295)
*Junior Tutorial and Seminar (Humanities 297)
*Senior Tutorial and Seminar (Humanities 298)

Interdisciplinary Courses

History of European Cinema as Visual Art (Art History 255)
History of American Cinema as Visual Art (Art History 256)
*Studies in the History of Film as a Visual Art (Hollywood Musicals) (Art History 355)
*Interdisciplinary Studies (Horror Classics: Fiction and Film) (Comparative Literature 295)
Film as Literature (English 273)
*Interdisciplinary Studies (Writer-Directors: Hitchcock, Fellini, Kubrick) (English 375)

*Seminar: Interdisciplinary Studies (The Hollywood Studio System) (English 478)
Proseminar in the Teaching of College English: Film Section (English 493)
French and Comparative Cinema I (French 288)
French and Comparative Cinema II (French 289)
Seminar in French and Comparative Cinema (French 452; Comparative
  Literature 472)
History of German Cinema (German 390)
*Film and History (Depression America and Its Films) (History 296)
Independent Film (Humanities 199)
The Japanese Cinema (Humanities 395)
Philosophy and Film (Philosophy 301)
Films of Ingmar Bergman (Scandinavian 390)
Cinema of Russia and East Europe (Slavic 319)
History of Comedy (Speech Communication 207, I)
Contemporary Comedy (Speech Communication 207, II)

Cinematography Courses

Introduction to Cinematography (Art 180)
Basic Cinematography (Art 280)
Cinematography (Art 388)

Undergraduate Concentration in Cinema Studies (Major)

Requirements (51–57 hours):

1. Acquire a knowledge of at least one foreign language sufficient to the student's program in film studies. In most cases, this requirement will exceed the
   college language requirement by six semester hours of study. The language
   and the level of proficiency will be determined in consultation with the option adviser.
2. An introductory course: English 104. (3 hours)
3. A two-semester general survey of world film: Humanities 261 and 262. (6 hours)
4. A course in film theory and criticism: Humanities 361. (3 hours)
5. At least one course in filmmaking: Art 180 or 280 or 388 or equivalent. (3 hours)
6. Substitutions for specific courses listed above will be approved by the option
   adviser only in exceptional cases.
7. At least 18 additional hours in film courses offered in individual departments
   in the School of Humanities. At least 9 of these hours must be in courses offered in foreign language departments and at least two languages must be
   represented in the total. (18 hours)
8. At least 12 additional hours of related courses in one or more of the following
   general fields: aesthetics, art or architectural history, communications,
   criticism, cultural anthropology, foreign language studies, linguistics, literature
   (fiction and/or drama), modern history, music, philosophy, photography,
   theater. Specific courses and sequences in these fields are to be approved at
   the discretion of the option adviser, except that courses that are eligible to
   satisfy requirement 7 may not be approved under requirement 8. (12 hours)
9. Three hours in the Junior Tutorial and Seminar, Humanities 297. This course
   will involve an independent research project in a field of cinema defined by
   the student and the submission of a substantial piece of writing growing out
   of this research. (3 hours)

10. Three hours in the Senior Tutorial and Seminar, Humanities 298. This course will involve the completion of a significant paper somewhat comparable to a senior honors thesis. (3 hours)

Teacher Education Minor in Cinema Studies

Requirements (24 hours):

1. An introductory course: English 104. (3 hours)
2. At least one course in filmmaking: Art 180 or 280 or 388 or equivalent. (3 hours)
3. The first half of a two-semester general survey of world film: Humanities 261. (3 hours)
4. Either the second half of the world film survey, Humanities 262, or a course in film theory and criticism, Humanities 361. (3 hours)
5. Three hours in the Junior Tutorial and Seminar, Humanities 297. This course will involve an independent research project in a field of cinema defined by the student and the submission of a substantial piece of writing growing out of this research.
6. Nine additional hours in cinema studies courses offered in departments in the School of Humanities. At least two departments must be represented in the total.

Film in the English Department:
The Wayne State Version

Joseph A. Gomez

Dept. responsible for the film program   Departments of English and Speech (but a
film major is only available through the speech department)

Full-time faculty in the dept. teaching film   2 (English)
3 (speech communication)

Enrollment policies
maximum class enrollment (if applicable)   75
minimum class enrollment   12
average class enrollment   30–35

Staffing
% of film courses taught by part-time faculty   English 15% Speech 25%
% taught by full-time instructors or lecturers   0%
% taught by asst., assoc., and full professors   85%/75%

Program size
# of students enrolled in the film program
in fall of 1982   330 (35 film studies majors)
# of undergraduate courses offered in the fall
term of 1982   7
# of courses at all levels offered in the program   17
# of students enrolled at the institution   29,775

At first viewing, the development of film courses in the Department of English at Wayne State University appears to imitate the clichéd script of an old B western. The powerful cattlemen have enjoyed the use of the open range for years. Suddenly a stranger, a sheepherder, comes to town. The cattlemen use force to cut off his use of the land. A bloody battle occurs. The members of the town take sides, and finally the sheriff is forced to restore order. When the smoke clears, we find that there is room for all, and the entire town prospers as a result. There are, however, enough interesting variations in the presentation of this plot to make the retelling of the Wayne State version worthwhile.

Wayne State's first film course, "Motion Picture Speech," was introduced in 1943 and was described in the university bulletin as "a detailed study of motion pictures as a means of influencing audiences." In the late 1940s Leonard Leone of the theater wing of the speech department introduced new courses called "Motion Pictures in the United States" and "History and Appreciation of the Motion Picture." By 1956, the courses entitled "Motion Picture Speech" and "Motion Pictures in the United States" were replaced by a fundamentals of filmmaking course and an advanced history and appreciation course. These courses were under the control of the theater area of the speech department until the mid-sixties, when an advanced film production class was added to the catalog and both filmmaking courses became part of the mass communications area of the speech department. The status quo prevailed until 1971. At that time the existing production courses were revised, and new courses were added in animation and cinematography techniques. All of these courses were listed, in turn, as part of the mass communications curriculum, but the history of film courses remained staffed and controlled by theater faculty.

During the so-called film boom of the late sixties and early seventies, other departments, most notably art and Romance languages, attempted to initiate film courses, but no sustained program was established by them. Various members of the English department also proposed that film courses be introduced in their department. The prevailing view, however, remained that film had no place in the English curriculum. After all, as some faculty members noted, even Ingmar Bergman had gone on record as indicating that film had nothing to do with literature. Also, I suspect that some professors were already nervous about the growing folklore and linguistics concentrations in a literature department. In any event, Wayne's English faculty moved slowly and cautiously in its consideration of the place of film in its curriculum. Finally, Marilyn Williamson, a former English department head who had become associate dean of liberal arts, committed herself to establishing a place for film in the department, and I was hired as a "film person" with a background both in film and literature.

Upon arriving at Wayne in September 1976, I proposed an introductory course in film aesthetics and a more advanced course that examined the multiple relationships between film and literature. The logic behind this sequence involved the idea that literature students needed a course to provide an introduction to cinematic techniques and methods of analysis before they could adequately discuss complex relationships between film and literature, but—perhaps because of declining enrollments throughout the university—the speech department perceived the proposal of an introductory film course as a direct threat to an area clearly under its control. The ensuing discussions about this issue were difficult and resulted in the withdrawal of the original course proposal and the formation of the Interdepartmental Committee on Film Studies, which I was asked to chair.

I then promptly proposed a new course entitled "Introduction to Film and Literature," and, because the course title contained the word "literature," the course was not challenged by the speech department. Former English department chairmen Edward Sharples and James Malek both agreed with the view (which Sergei Eisenstein proved years ago) that some of the basic techniques of filmmaking were influenced by literature. Both men also supported my contentions that an instructor may use similar modes of analysis when teaching verbal or visual narratives and that film courses and not simply an adaptation course had a place in the department. As a result, under the general rubric of "Themes and Techniques in Film and Literature," I was allowed to teach courses in "Experimental Narrative Structure in Film," "Film and Fusion of the Arts," and "The Subversive Film as Art."

While faculty members at other colleges and universities often have to battle an unsympathetic administration over the development of film courses, at Wayne State University the situation was reversed. In 1976, Dean Williamson charged the newly formed committee on film studies to develop additional courses and to work for university-wide cooperation at all levels. As a result, during its first year of existence, the committee approved two film and literature courses proposed by the English department and a documentary film course proposed by the speech department. Also, the "History of Film" course was restructured and divided into two courses—"The Silent Period" and "The Sound Period."

The formation of the Interdepartmental Committee on Film Studies also provided an opportunity for faculty members with similar interests to meet to confront significant issues aside from those of curriculum. For instance, the practical problems of running film courses in a large, unbelievably bureaucratic university were discussed. Though little was accomplished concerning difficulties with facilities or in altering Wayne State's practice of charging departments for the use of films that belong to the university's own collection, progress was made in areas of shared rentals and cooperation with student film groups in the use of films on campus. Finally, since most of the members of the committee, including those in the mass communications area, found few people within their home departments who shared their interests in film, the committee itself fostered collegiality.

Indeed, the commitment of this committee to building a strong, university-wide program in film has reduced suspicions and territorial concerns. At present, each department is involved with the development of courses related to its own unique approach to film. The Department of Speech Communication, Theater, and Journalism focuses on film production and film history, the Department of Romance and Germanic Languages is concerned with cultural aspects of European national cinemas, and film courses in the Department of English deal with criticism, theory, and film and literature. Still, the ultimate goal is a university-wide program in which the student can profit from the unique approaches to film found in various departments throughout the university.

In the fall of 1980, Wayne State University moved to the semester system, and as a result of this change in the calendar, the film studies committee took the opportunity to make drastic revisions in the film curriculum. In the English department, the "literature" tag incorporated into the titles of film courses was dropped altogether, except in the titles of adaptation courses, and upper-level courses entitled "Styles and Genres in Film" and "Topics in Film" were added to the department's offerings. The most significant change, however, was the cross-listing of the lower-level "Introduction to Film" course by the English and speech departments. The success of these new courses in general and the introductory course in particular provided opportunities to create even more new courses and to establish yet another cross-listed course. Speech has added a course in scriptwriting, English has developed "Film Criticism and Theory," and "History of Film" is now cross-listed by English and speech.

In April 1982, a crucial step toward a truly interdepartmental film program was accomplished when the Liberal Arts Faculty Council unanimously approved a proposal for a film studies minor cosponsored by the Departments of Speech and English. In turn, this development has encouraged the Romance and Germanic languages department to become directly involved, with English and speech, in the creation of a university-wide film program, and discussions concerning the revision and possible cross-listing of even more courses have been initiated.

The successful development of film courses in the English department at Wayne State University has come about because of the work of the Interdepartmental Film Studies Committee to improve the quality of film education within the university and because of the support of the former and present English department chairpersons. Instead of simply allowing for the scheduling of random courses in film to attract students outside of the department, Sharples, Malek, and Williamson argued for a gradual but consistent progression. Although there are no prerequisites for any of the film courses offered in the English department, English 245: "Introduction to Film" has been treated as a "feeder" course to those at a higher numerical level. No attempt, however, has been made to turn this course into a depersonalized, massive lecture class, and thus multiple sections are offered each semester. The enrollment for individual sections has varied between thirty-five and seventy-five students, and often this course contains the highest section enrollment of any course offered in English during a given semester. Usually three upper-level film courses are scheduled per year, and the topics for these courses are generally repeated only after two-year intervals. Of these more specialized courses, "Literature into Film" is repeated with the most regularity, but "Topics in Film: Subversive Film as Art" has attracted the largest enrollment (75 students) thus far for a single section.

All the film courses in the English department are structured on the premise that film is a unique form of creative expression that can and should be studied with the insight and intensity given to literary texts. The classes themselves, as a result, emphasize discussion of how filmmakers choose to solve artistic problems generated by the specific nature of the medium, how aesthetic form, in the best films, reveals thematic content, and how audiences should understand the subtle nuances of aural-visual patterning in order to appreciate the complexities of an artistic work and/or to guard themselves against insidious manipulative devices.

Depth, as much as breadth, is the key word for these courses, and, therefore, multiple screenings of films are arranged for students. Every film is seen in class (usually on Monday or Tuesday), and a two-hour class discussion follows on Wednesday or Thursday. During the week that the film is on campus as many screenings as possible are arranged—either through the student cinema group or through special screenings projected by a student assistant from the English department. Because of the strong emphasis on multiple viewings and the detailed analysis of sequences from films during class discussion, the English department has made a strong commitment to purchasing a core collection of feature films.

Admittedly, some Wayne State students are tempted to fulfill their university English requirements by taking film courses in order to avoid the reading and writing assignments found in the traditional literature courses. Reading assignments, however, are crucial to every film course taught in the English department, and writing assignments rival those of any undergraduate literature course in length, number, and level of difficulty. For instance, a recent genre offering entitled "The Nightmare World" examined how Gothic fiction, German expressionism, and surrealism helped to shape the horror film. Reading and/or writing assignments involving these respective areas supplemented the screening and discussion of almost all the films in the course.

The description of the film courses that follows does not include expected future offerings or proposals for an interdepartmental film major; instead it presents an accurate picture of Wayne State University's film program as of fall 1982.

Courses in Film
Film studies at Wayne State University are coordinated by an interdisciplinary faculty committee of the College of Liberal Arts. Courses in film are listed in the 1982–84 *Bulletin* in the following departments:

English Language and Literature
ENG 120: Film and Literature   Film and its relation to literature. (4 credits)
ENG 245: Introduction to Film (Same as SPF 201)   Examination of film techniques and the basic methods of film analysis. (4 credits)
ENG 246: History of Film (Same as SPF 202)   (4 credits)
ENG 504: Film Criticism and Theory   Study of the attitudes of important film critics and theorists from Sergei Eisenstein to the present. (3 credits)
ENG 505: Literature into Film   Ways of adapting literary works to film form. Focus on the artistic and practical problems of transforming literature to film. (3 credits)
ENG 506: Styles and Genres in Film   Study of significant works within selected genres: the western, the horror film, comedies. Emphasis on styles of particular directors. Topics to be announced in Schedule of Classes. (3 credits, 9 maximum)
ENG 507: Topics in Film   Topics such as "Film and Fusion of the Arts" and "Subversive Film as Art." To be announced in Schedule of Classes. (3 credits, 9 maximum)

Romance and Germanic Languages
FRE 515: French Cinema as Literature   Study of diverse aspects of French cinema, e.g., social realism, poetic cinema, or specific filmmakers, with reference to contemporary trends in literature and society. (3 credits, 6 maximum)
ITA 315: Aspects of Italian Cinema   Major developments in the Italian cinema from the origins to the present. Knowledge of Italian not required. Topics to be announced in the Schedule of Classes. (3 credits, 6 maximum)
ITA 515: Advanced Study of Italian Cinema   Concentrated study of specific trends or the development of individual directors. Topics to be announced in the Schedule of Classes. (3 credits, 6 maximum)

Speech Communication, Theater, and Journalism

SPF 201: Introduction to Film (ENG 245) (4 credits)

SPF 202: History of Film Critical study of the motion picture as a modern visual art; screening and analysis of representative fiction films to illustrate important historical periods and genres. (4 credits)

SPF 502: Studies in Film History Analysis of the development of a specific film genre, a director, or other historical aspects of the motion picture. Topics to be announced in the Schedule of Classes. (4 credits, 12 maximum)

SPF 506: Documentary and Nonfiction Film Study of the nonfiction film made for a social, cultural, or political purpose; screening and analysis of selected nonfiction films intended for theater and television audiences. (4 credits)

SPF 525: Scriptwriting Principles and techniques of writing for motion pictures. Analysis and study of professionally written scripts. Exercise in writing documentary and dramatic film scripts. (3 credits, 9 maximum)

SPF 543: Film Production I Introduction to principles of cinematography (including cameras, lenses, film stock, pictorial composition, and lighting) and editing (including screen continuity and sound interlock); projects utilize Super-8mm and 16mm equipment. (4 credits)

SPF 544: Film Production II Continuation of SPF 543. All aspects of sound motion-picture production including emphasis on scripting, budgeting, shooting and direction, postproduction, sound mixing, and AB roll editing. (4 credits)

SPF 546: Motion Picture Animation Techniques Theory and application of various forms and styles of film animation. (3 credits)

SPF 852: Seminar in Film Topics will vary with instructor. (3 credits, 9 maximum)

Undergraduate Film Studies Major

A film major is available in the mass communications area of the speech department. It requires basic courses in film history, theory, and criticism as well as in film production. At the advanced level, it encourages students to follow their own interests as film scholars or filmmakers. The degree is a Bachelor of Arts. The required courses (25–26 semester credit hours) are:

SPF 201: Introduction to Film (ENG 245)

SPR 201: Survey of Mass Communications *or* Mass Media Appreciation and Criticism (SPR 301)

SPF 202: History of Film (ENG 246)

SPR 221: Writing for Radio-Television-Film

SPF 543: Film Production I

SPF 502: Studies in Film History *or* Film Production II (SPF 544)

SPF 506: Documentary and Nonfiction Film *or* Mass Communication and Society (SPR 551)

An additional ten semester credit hours must be elected from the film courses available in the College of Liberal Arts, and an expanded liberal arts requirement in the humanities–social sciences group must be satisfied (in part with additional film courses, if the student wishes).

Undergraduate Film Studies Minor

The film studies minor is cosponsored by the speech and English departments and is administered by the Interdepartmental Film Studies Committee. It requires

SPF 201/ENG 245 and a minimum of fifteen credits to be chosen from the following courses:

SPF 202/ENG 246: History of Film
SPF 502: Studies in Film History
SPF 506: Documentary and Nonfiction Film
SPF 543: Film Production I
ENG 504: Film Theory and Criticism
ENG 505: Literature into Film
ENG 506: Styles and Genres in Film
ENG 507: Topics in Film
ITA 315: Aspects of Italian Cinema

Graduate Film Studies

M.A. and Ph.D. degrees are offered by all three liberal arts departments giving courses in film, and a master's essay or thesis or a Ph.D. dissertation dealing with film may be undertaken in any of the departments if it addresses research questions and utilizes research methodologies appropriate to the discipline of the major department. A graduate major in film as such is available within the mass communications area of the speech department, although course work in other areas of speech communication and in another department (preferably English) will be required.

Film Programs in the University Neighborhood

Three programs regularly schedule screenings of important contemporary American and foreign films and classics for public audiences in the campus area. The Wayne Cinema Guild is a student organization that announces its schedule of screenings at the beginning of each semester. The Detroit Film Theatre attracts large audiences to films at the auditorium of the Detroit Institute of Arts each Friday, Saturday, and Sunday. It charges a modest admission, as does the Cass City Cinema, which schedules its screenings on Fridays and Saturdays in the Unitarian Church, Cass Avenue at Forest Street.

Purdue University.

In fact, cinema is too large, too complex, too comprehensive and eclectic to be confined to any one department or discipline. Specialists from many disciplines may usefully approach the cinema by applying their own specialized tools of analysis. Sociologists such as Garth Jowett and Ian Jarvie, for example, may approach the movies as social criticism. A philosopher such as Stanley Cavell may usefully reflect "on the ontology of film." Arthur M. Schlesinger, Jr., has observed that the movies offer "a varied and complex wilderness of evidence for the modern historian." Specialized journals such as *Jump Cut* and *Cinéaste* explore the political implications of cinema. Experimental films are analyzed by art historians in *Artforum* and by specialists in photography in *Afterimage*. Stanley Kauffmann, the film critic of the *New Republic*, is also a drama critic, and his evaluations of film acting are therefore enhanced by his expertise and by his experience in drama. Scholar-critics trained in the discipline of English may begin the serious teaching of film by applying to narrative films their specialized training in narrative theory, dramatic construction, point of view, or character design and development and by considering the particular problems of adapting or transforming literary and dramatic works into cinema.

And yet there are colleagues in the profession who still regard those of us interested in cinema with skepticism, if not suspicion. "Movies" may encompass the work of Ingmar Bergman and Federico Fellini, but by and large they still represent insidious popular culture to many who are elitist and conservative in their orientation and training. My remarks at a special conference, "Film and the Humanities," sponsored by the Rockefeller Foundation in New York on 19 October 1976, still have relevance: "Those who use film are seen as less-than-serious scholars and are thought by some to be demeaning the 'genuine' humanistic issues with which intellectuals should be concerned. This disdain often translates into negative sanctions when tenure and promotion decisions are made. Part of the problem may be the absence of 'visual literacy' among many humanists; it is very hard to break ground against an overwhelming bias in favor of the book" (2).

Perhaps not all of these criticisms apply to the situation at Salisbury State College, but most certainly the study of literature there is believed to be the primary function of the English department. "All concentrations are parts of a whole," the chairman wrote in a memo to faculty dated 23 January 1979, "and the literature requirement in the major accompanying each concentration suggts that the matrix in the major is literature, complemented by related areas of study." Here, as elsewhere, there would indeed seem to be "an overwhelming bias in favor of the book," even though the memo goes on to state that "there is no hierarchy based on superiority; there are simply differences in kind." If one teaches a course entitled "Literature and Film," that, obviously, will be considered an appropriate "literature" course that students may use to satisfy the general education requirements at the college. But what if one teaches a course entitled "The Cinema of Ingmar Bergman" or a genre course that deals with westerns? There is a need, certainly, for English courses in literature and film, or drama and film, or Shakespeare and film, and many such courses have been designed and are in operation. But it also makes sense to study the humanistic substance of films that may not derive from literary sources, for film should not be used merely to illustrate classics of literature. A humanities course that takes as its substance the cinema of Ingmar Bergman, to take one unassailable example, makes as much sense as one concentrating upon the plays of Shakespeare or Eugene O'Neill. A course I taught in Ingmar Bergman in fact carried "literature" credit; but, even in the case of this "unassailable" auteur, the credit was not granted without considerable departmental discussion. Fortunately, Bergman's screenplays were available in print and could be picked up and read. Again, the "overwhelming bias in favor of the book."

I taught the first "Introduction to Film" course at Salisbury State College during the spring term of 1972 with sixty students enrolled. Because of my programming experience as a graduate student, because I knew who the 16mm distributors were and what they had to offer and, most important, how to dicker with them, I was able to run this first film course at Salisbury State on a meager support budget of about $400. (A normal support budget these days for a fifteen-week semester would run from $1,000 to $1,200, depending on one's ability to bargain and one's willingness to compromise.) The rental budget itself can be a barrier since normal departments of English are probably not used to requesting such luxuries. At Salisbury I have managed to augment the academic budget with an additional budget from our College Center. For the last several years I have organized and operated an International Film Series for the director of the College Center, choosing the films I teach in my courses. This represents an additional expense of time and energy—booking the films, writing, copy editing, laying out, and proofreading the cultural affairs brochure, projecting the films, and mailing them back to distributors—but the advantages far outweigh the time so donated. I have been able to bring to my students films that would ordinarily be beyond my reach: Resnais's *Je t'aime, je t'aime*, for example, Rohmer's *Die Marquise von O. . . .*, Fassbinder's *Merchant of Four Seasons* and *Effi Briest*, Herzog's *Stroszek* and *Aquirre, the Wrath of God*, to say nothing of nearly all the available works of Ingmar Bergman, François Truffaut, Peter Watkins, Nicolas Roeg, and Wim Wenders.

One other colleague in the English department, Thomas L. Erskine, shares with me the main responsibility of teaching our film courses. Together, the two of us also founded *Literature/Film Quarterly*, now entering its eleventh year of publication. The story of the establishment of *Literature/Film Quarterly* is told in some detail by J. M. Welsh in "Periodical Frustrations," which appeared in the *AFI Education Newsletter* (6.2 [1982]: 1–2, 8). In his first year at Salisbury State College Erskine served as chairman of the English department. He performed his duties as chairman so successfully that in his second year he was promoted to academic dean. His programs and projects were therefore favored by the president of the college, who agreed to a subsidy for the establishment of a cinema journal, *Literature/Film Quarterly*. Erskine's tenure as dean provided enough time for the journal to get through the first few years, when subscriptions are relatively difficult to come by. After the first two years, however, subscriptions had grown to about five hundred, then considered by the Modern Language Association to be the average number of subscribers for specialized journals in the fields of language and literature.

Given this interest and these circumstances, it was only natural that film courses would be allowed to thrive and proliferate. Since most of these courses proved to be popular with students, there was no problem at all in getting them approved and in the catalog. With Erskine serving as dean, moreover, there was no difficulty in getting budgetary support for the film courses that were offered. When Erksine stepped down from the deanship and returned to the teaching faculty, funding for the film courses, which by and large were demonstrably popular, continued.

Funding for *Literature/Film Quarterly* also continued, but steps were necessarily taken to economize the operation. Typesetting and layout had thereafter to be done "in-house," which put a great deal of additional work onto the editors. Since no release time from teaching is given to compensate for this labor, the continued operation of the journal over the past three years has been difficult, if not onerous. The editors have continued their work, however, because they consider it worthwhile in terms of professional service and personal satisfaction.

The first "Literature and Film" course, with fifty-seven enrolled students, was taught during the fall term of 1972. Both Erskine and I have team-taught film courses with colleagues from other disciplines. I team-taught a course called "Mass Media and Society" with a colleague from communication arts and thereafter turned the course over to his department. With a colleague from the philosophy department I have team-taught "Film and the Revolutionary Ethic" and "The Films and Philosophy of the New Wave." Erskine has team-taught two courses with the chairman of the sociology department—"Film and Social Issues" and "The Hollywood Myth."

The two most popular courses we teach are "Introduction to Film" (which enrolls nearly forty students every semester) and "Literature and Film" (which commonly runs to over eighty preregistered students). Up until 1980, the largest sections I had taught, both courses in genre films (one on screen comedy, the other on the western), enrolled more than one hundred students per section. The last time "Film History" was offered (spring 1979), seventy-five students enrolled. These courses have set enrollment records for the department. I believe they help to explain why enrollments in English courses have increased, even though the number of English majors has correspondingly decreased. (To make class loads fair and equitable, however, we have recently established a limit of fifty students a section.)

The largest English and film course ever offered at Salisbury State College was the "Literature and Film" course (a 300-level offering that serves to satisfy the general education literature requirement at the college) for the spring term of 1980. Preregistration figures for this course in the late fall of 1979 indicated that 121 students were interested in taking this course, and it was clear that even more students were likely to add the course during the regular registration period. Clearly, this was more than a single faculty member could be expected to handle.

As a consequence, an important precedent was established. My course was split into two sections, and Erskine, having canceled one of his spring term courses, took on half of the burden. Final registration figures placed approximately 160 students in this class. All these students would meet in the same auditorium to view the films; the class would then split into two separate sections for lectures and discussion. It has been my experience that class discussion is possible—to a degree—in a class of eighty students. A system of computer grading was designed to facilitate weekly quizzes on the assigned readings. Beyond this, two papers and a final examination were required to earn credit for the course.

The English department at Salisbury State College is an eclectic one serving many interests. There is at present no film major at the college, though a number of film and media courses are regularly offered. English majors could only elect a rather vaguely defined concentration in film, as they could also elect concentrations in folklore, linguistics, journalism, or creative writing. There was, before

1980, a two-track major in English at Salisbury State College, one for "regular" English majors, the other for secondary education English majors. Training in English primarily meant training in literature.

The eclectic nature of the department would be beter served, I argued in 1979, if the department were to offer three types of major, splitting what was then the "regular" English major into two categories: literature majors (who would concentrate in the study of literature and retain the present foreign language requirement) and English majors (who would concentrate in film, folklore, linguistics, journalism, creative writing, or any intelligent combination thereof, and who would not necessarily be held to the current foreign language requirement). Twelve to fifteen hours in any given concentration might then be identified as a minor. (It ought to be possible, I reasoned, to major in English and minor in film and media.)

Given these options, the literature major would be as solid and traditional as ever and would well serve the student who might be bound for graduate school. The English major, on the other hand, would serve generalists, exposing them to the department's strengths but sparing them some of the obstacles. This kind of diversity, I believed, would better serve both the student body (which had changed over the last decade in motivation and temperament) and the English faculty.

The department had fallen victim to its own diversity. Without realizing exactly what had happened, it had become greater than its parts. Those who favored literature were in the majority and in control of department policy. Others in the minority wings had begun to feel alienated. Some felt their contributions were not properly understood or appreciated. Factions began to form. By January 1980 it was clear that some kind of reasonable compromise had to be reached for the good of the department. As a consequence, the department was restructured so as to better reflect its diversity. This restructuring roughly approximated the proposal I had suggested to the department in 1979.

Between 1971 and 1980 film courses proliferated within the English department at Salisbury State. But even though students could take a variety of different courses, administratively they could only be identified as English majors. This was to change on 17 January 1980, when the fifteen-member department, by nearly unanimous vote, agreed to restructure the department in such a way that students would be recognized according to their concentrations—English and literature, English and linguistics, English and folklore, and English and film. Students electing the English and film concentration in future will be required to take English 101-102 (the six-hour freshman English sequence required of all students), nine additional hours of literature courses (but particularly those involving narrative literature), "Introduction to Film" (English 214), "Film History" (English 321), "Literature and Film" (English 322), "Film Genre," "Major Directors," and two courses taught in the communication arts department—"Mass Media Society" and "Elements of Filmmaking." Beyond these thirty-six required hours for the English and film major, students may choose elective courses. Those students particularly interested in foreign directors and movements (such as the *nouvelle vague* or *das neue Kino*) will be urged to take coordinate courses in foreign languages and literatures but not required to do so. The foreign language requirement, long held in effect for English majors after it had been dropped by other departments, was not considered essential for English and film majors who were primarily interested in the American cinema and films of the silent era, though language study is still strongly recommended for those interested in foreign films.

Though the bias in our department has definitely been towards literature, the department has been supportive of the film courses offered. The major remaining contention settles upon the question of which courses offered by the department will satisfy the general education program requirements of the college. All students here are made to take an additional three hours of literature over and beyond the six-hour freshman English requirement. Some members of the department would like to see any English course as being appropriate to settle this additional requirement. I am not in fact certain that some distinctions should not be made; but it does seem to me strange that a course in "Western Literature" (i.e., cowboy novels) would satisfy this requirement, whereas a course in "Western Movies"—heavy on Ford, Hawks, and Peckinpah—would not. On the other hand, the idea of teaching cinema in the English department has never to my knowledge been seriously questioned. The conclusion is obvious: by and large the relationship so far has been a harmonious one.

Works Cited

Canudo, Ricciotto. "Manifesto of the Seven Arts." Trans. Steven Philip Kramer. *Literature/Film Quarterly* 3.3 (1975): 252-54.
Ruhe, Edward L. "Film: The 'Literary' Approach." *Literature/Film Quarterly* 1.1 (1973): 76-83.
Welsh, James Michael. "Narrative Summary." *Film and the Humanities*. Ed. John O'Connor. New York: Rockefeller Foundation, 1977, 1-12.

Courses

English 214: Introduction to Film (Welsh or Erskine)   A study of what film is and can become, of technique, the roles of the director, cameraman, writer. Screening of selected film classics (sound and silent, features and shorts) to demonstrate the process of understanding movies.

English 321: Film History (Welsh)   A survey of the cinema from Griffith and Gance to Hitchcock and Welles. The emphasis will fall on American movies from the silent period through the coming of sound to the rise of the studio system, with some attention given to parallel developments in other countries.

English 322: Literature and Film (Erskine or Welsh)   This course will study the process of adapting novels, short stories, and plays into film. Although the course may be counted as an English elective, the literature surveyed here is by no means limited to works originally in English; but the main problem is to examine how literary originals can be "translated" or "transformed" into cinema.

English 490: Topics in English: Critical Reviewing (Welsh)   The purpose of this course is to give students practical experience writing short critical reviews (mainly of films and books). Students will write eight to ten reviews with the idea that some of their work may see publication in local papers. The grade for the course will be determined by the number and quality of reviews written. This course is not for beginners. It can be recommended, however, for students who especially enjoy writing about films and talking about the cinema, who care enough to think critically about what the elements of a "good" or "great" film must be, and who are sufficiently daring and confident to write for or speak to an audience.

English 325: Studies in Film: Screen Comedy (Welsh)   A survey of various modes of comic and satiric motion pictures: from what James Agee has called "Comedy's Greatest Era" to *Dr. Strangelove*, from Sennett and Chaplin, Keaton, Langdon, and Lloyd through "Screwball Comedy" to Truffaut, Fellini, and Bergman (yes, Bergman). The main text will be Gerald Mast's *The Comic Mind*. Other readings in comic theory will be assigned: Bergson's essay "Laughter," for example, and Meredith's "Comedy."

English 490: Topics in English: Major European Directors (Welsh)   This course will cover at least six or seven major figures of the European cinema—Bergman, Fellini, Buñuel, Eisenstein, Hitchcock, Godard, and Truffaut. Representative films will be shown and discussed in depth.

English 300: Studies in English: Shakespeare on Film (Welsh)   There is a vital cinematic tradition of Shakespeare on film capturing for posterity a valuable record of Shakespearean production: the purpose of this course is to study the plays of Shakespeare in the light of that tradition. Particular attention will be paid to the relevant distinctions between theater and film, but the major emphasis will certainly fall upon the plays themselves.

English 325: Studies in Film: The Cinema of Ingmar Bergman (Welsh)   A survey of nine of the most recent and significant films of the thirty-four made by Sweden's greatest filmmaker. Students will read criticism by three of Bergman's best critics—John Simon, Birgitta Steene, and Robin Wood (all required)—and will also be directed to other critical reviews.

English 342: Filmwriting Workshop (Whall)   Practice in the craft of writing film scripts using both original and adapted material. Discussion of scripts, camera techniques, shot analysis.

English 300: Women in Film (Erskine)   Women in film—sexual, psychological, social roles. Garbo, Dietrich, Fonda, Monroe; directors Wertmueller, Zetterling. Weekly screenings and discussions.

English 300: American Film Genre: Westerns and Gangsters (Welsh)   Will historically study in depth two types of American movies, each depending upon given formulas and developing "traditions," beginning, e.g., with Wm. S. Hart, Tom Mix, and John Ford, through psychological westerns such as *High Noon* and *Shane* to *The Wild Bunch* and what has been called the post-western. The parallel development of the gangster film will be examined as a sort of reverse image of the western, though both genres, to be sure, involve men with guns.

English 300/Philosophy 310: Film, Politics, and the Revolutionary Ethic (Welsh and Kane)   Philosophical themes surrounding our political existence are contained in and transmitted by the medium of film. We will examine film as an ideological tool, a means of moving minds and of nurturing emotions. We will study films of protest and propaganda by Eisenstein, Gance, Costa-Gavras, Godard, Bertolucci, and others.

English 300: Avant-Garde and Documentaries (Erskine):   The experimental and avant-garde film from the dada films of Buñuel to the underground films of Baillie, Brakhage, and Connor; the documentary film from Grierson and Flaherty to Wiseman and Leacock.

English 300/Sociology 490: The Hollywood Myth (Erskine and Bosserman)   Hollywood as mirror, as Babylon, as shaper of American cuture, and as social milieu. Topics include the studio system, the fanzines, the "dream factory," movie theaters, impact on writers. Novels, essays, and films about Hollywood.

English 300: Women Film Directors (Erskine)   A study of the major films directed by women. Begins with the films of Ida Lupino and includes Sontag, Arzner, Zetterling, Silver, Darling, and Wertmueller.

English 300/Sociology 490: Film and Social Issues (Erskine and Bosserman)   Screening and discussion of Hollywood films that address social problems of alcoholism, drug abuse, education, racism, juvenile delinquency, and aging.

English 300/Philosophy 310: The Films and Philosophy of the New Wave (Welsh and Kane)   Cinematic and philosophical study of the French New Wave—those who influenced it (Bazin, Astruc, Renoir, and Gance) and the auteur filmmakers who created it (Truffaut, Godard, etc.).

Communication Arts 300: The Elements of Filmmaking (Auch)   As a member of a production team, the student participates in the making of a story film, practicing the principles of pictorial continuity: the shot, the sequence, editing, acting, and directing.

Education 416: Filmmaking in Educational Settings (Wilby)   Designed to foster filmmaking skills in school situations. Students work in teams planning and producing Super-8mm films. Emphasis given to animation, live-acting, and montage techniques.

Film Studies at the University of Nevada, Las Vegas

Hart Wegner

Dept. responsible for the film program	Interdisciplinary program	
Full-time faculty in the program		7
Enrollment policies		
maximum class enrollment (if applicable)		N/A
minimum class enrollment		12
average class enrollment		40
Staffing		
% of film courses taught by part-time faculty		0%
% taught by full-time instructors or lecturers		0%
% taught by asst., assoc., and full professors		100%
Program size		
# of students enrolled in the film program in fall of 1979		6 majors
# of courses offered in the fall term of 1979		5
# of courses at all levels offered in the program		15
# of students enrolled at the institution		10,000

The purpose and goal of this film studies program is to aid the students in acquiring a form of visual literacy. The study of film, its history, aesthetics, genres, and narrative methods, provides visual instruction, enabling students to cope intelligently and critically with an increasingly visual environment. Since greater parts of our learning processes have become visual too, Marshall McLuhan's dictum of the 1960s "The movie, radio, and TV: classroom without walls" seems even more applicable to the 1980s.

Recognizing the need for film studies and actually initiating such a program at the University of Nevada proved to be two different things. Steps had to be taken to make the planned program administratively acceptable and interesting. Various avenues toward establishing a film studies program on this campus were undertaken in the early 1970s with mixed results.

Development of the University of Nevada, Las Vegas, Film Studies Program

The first film courses at this university were offered in cooperation with the student government. The regular student film series incorporated into its Wednesday night program films selected by the instructor. Since these films were rented by Student Activities, the film courses were freed from the financial burden of more expensive pictures. These initial film courses attracted enough students to ensure success (in administrative terms), but certain problems caused the termination of the cooperation of student government and film studies. The quality of the screenings, held in the ballroom of the Student Union, was not conducive to a serious study of film. Noise, disruptions, and poor projection were frustrating to the faculty as well as to the film students. The film selection committee grew reluctant to commit student funds for the showing of films deemed "instructional"; the money came from student activity fees and was earmarked to provide entertainment.

The most serious problem that disturbed this arrangement is one inherent in the structure of student governments: annual elections. These not only change the people in individual positions but alter also the philosophy of the various committees overseeing the disbursement of the not inconsiderable monies available to student governments. Since film course planning takes considerable lead time, those students who enthusiastically supported the early planning were no longer in office when their promises needed to be redeemed. The reluctance of student officers to honor financial obligations incurred by their predecessors finally endangered the film studies' credit ratings with motion picture distributors.

Other avenues had to be found to make film courses economically viable. Film studies courses, more than any others in the humanities, require money beyond the salary of the instructor for their survival. The cost of acquiring and maintaining projection equipment and the cost of renting films make a beginning film studies program a particularly difficult enterprise.

Bargaining with film distributors and renting films in quantity, essential to reduce the cost of rentals, were made impossible through the peculiar film ordering system at this university. Individual purchase orders had to be filed for each film, and in each case the list price was charged. In order to reduce the cost of film rentals, other means had to be found. The possibility of a laboratory fee, a usual means of income in film studies programs, was rejected by the administration. As a result, the creation of a permanent film library was pursued, and funds were allocated for this development through the Department of English, the coordinator of film studies, and the dean of the College of Arts and Letters. For the time being the films were housed in various locations, depending on the source of financing.

In order to ensure professional handling, storage, cataloging, and distribution, the university library was approached. The curator of the nonbook collection of the Dickinson Library agreed to incorporate film into the long-range planning of his department. An annual sum of $2,500 (over a period of four years) was guaranteed for the purchase of 16mm film to augment the existing film collection, which was unified and transferred in turn to the university library. The decision of which films to purchase rests with the Film Studies Committee of the College of Arts and Letters.

Aside from the funds made available through the library, additional films and video cassettes are bought from funds in the office of the dean of the College of Arts and Letters and from the remaining balance in the rental budget at the end of the fiscal year (funding for all film courses for the academic year 1981–82 was $4,870). From these combined sources, over a hundred films and excerpts of feature films have so far been gathered in the film studies collection in the university library. These films have become the "arsenal" of film studies, ensuring the survival of the program even in the case of rental budget cuts. It may appear that undue emphasis is placed here on the bothersome question of funding, but, as is the case with film production, without money there are no films for film studies courses.

The argument advanced to launch the first film courses was that if written literature is taught through a succession of grades and classes, then it is of equal importance to teach film, a complex amalgam of literature, art, music, drama, architecture, and a variety of technical arts and crafts. The first film course was titled "Film and Literature." The title indicates in which direction film studies at this university was to develop, through choice as well as necessity. Because of sufficient student interest, this course was transferred into the regular English curriculum, at first under the cover of a utility course, "Themes in Literaure," with the subtitle "Film and Literature." The success of this course brought a demand for other film courses that were offered at first in the departments of English and Foreign Languages. These departments were to remain the mainstay of the film studies program in terms of financial support and the share of the faculty teaching load.

The distribution of film courses to individual departments was based on the availability, background, interest, and knowledge of individual instructors. The first film courses were taught by a professor with a background in comparative literature, and these new film courses were considered an extension of his assigned comparative literature courses. Comparative literature, its scope and its methods of research and instruction, became a model for the fledgling film courses. Film was treated never as an illustration of literature but as, in Weisstein's phrase, a "conglomerate implicating literature" (161) and thus amenable to literary methods of analysis and interpretation. This basic philosophical consideration and the resulting pedagogical approach are best illustrated in their application in one of our film courses.

"Drama and Film of German Expressionism" (listed as Foreign Languages 441 and cross-listed as an upper-division German course as well as a Group II film studies course) is actually a misnomer, as many film course titles were that had to be accepted by curriculum committees before the official recognition of film studies; it was then essential to stress the relation of film to an established discipline. To be sure, the varied influences of the theater are studied—the playwrights of the movement from Strindberg and Wedekind to Kaiser, the innovative stage directors (Jessner, Reinhardt, Piscator, and Brecht), and the actors with established theatrical styles—but this is done without slighting the contributions of the painters, poets, philosophers, and programmatic writers. Expressionistic film is traced from its beginning in Stellan Rye's *Student of Prague* (1913) through its main period with *The Cabinet of Dr. Caligari*, *The Golem*, *Backstairs*, *Nosferatu*, *The Last Laugh*, and *Metropolis* to Sternberg's *The Blue Angel*. For the student, film emerges as one art among others from the cultural and historical realities of the Weimar Republic.

The other concern of this course is to trace the spreading of thematic and stylistic elements of German cinematic expressionism through the films of emigrant directors and cinematographers (Lang, Freund, Ulmer, and Siodmak in particular) and in the careers of those directors who emulated particulars of that style, such as Whale, Reed, Welles, Dmytryk, and others.

The substructure for this interdisciplinary approach to film studies is formed by two courses that establish film's historical roots, its visual vocabulary, and its cross-disciplinary influences: "Introduction to Film" (English department) and "Language of Film" (foreign languages department).

The Film Studies Program at the University of Nevada, Las Vegas, Today

Although the basis of scholarship and instruction is comparative and literary, a study of the technical aspects and problems of filmmaking is considered essential for our students. To teach film production on a professional scale at this time would make the film studies program so expensive that its administrative support would be jeopardized. Purchases even of the necessary 16mm cameras and editing equipment for two courses go beyond the available funds. Because of this, the focus of film studies at the University of Nevada, Las Vegas, continues to be scholarly, emphasizing the heritage of national film productions, the various genre studies, and artistic and political movements through courses in several different departments.

Film instruction in the foreign languages department is divided into general film courses, such as "The Language of Film" (instruction in film technology and analysis) and "Continental Film" (a survey of European movements) and courses in French and German film.

The history department offers one permanent course, "History of the Russian Film." A course in the directorial career of Sergei Eisenstein is offered at irregular intervals.

The art department offers courses in beginning and advanced "personal" filmmaking rather than the preprofessional instruction available at the University of Southern California and the University of California, Los Angeles (both of which are relatively close to Las Vegas). Filmmaking as personal expression (or, as the catalog reads, "Art Filmmaking") utilizes Super-8mm equipment that allows these courses to be offered at a fraction of the cost of a course geared to 16mm production. This is merely a temporary solution, and future growth of the program (dependent on future financing) will provide an opportunity to upgrade the equipment to 16mm production.

The Department of Communications Studies offers courses in beginning and advanced television production, which can fulfill the production requirement for film studies majors. At present, both the television production and filmmaking courses are hampered by equipment needs.

English department film course offerings range from "Introduction to Film" (a lower-division class) to upper-division histories of the American and British cinema. The English department curriculum also includes comparative courses, such as "Film and Literature" and "The American Hero in Film and Literature." A course titled "Genre Studies in Film" allows for the teaching of specialized courses in the western, comedy, and other clearly defined areas.

The course "Politics and Film" is taught by a team from the Department of Political Science and will eventually be supplemented by a course now being planned, "Films and Society," which will be offered by the Department of Sociology.

The proximity of Las Vegas to Hollywood allows guest lecturers from the film industry to enrich instruction at a rather nominal cost. For example, the animation artists Chuck Jones and Walter Lantz have lectured here several times on the history of the American film. The university library, thanks to these lecturers, houses an animation collection of more than 100,000 drawings, background paintings, timing sheets, and musical scores for seventeen complete animated films.

During the ten years courses in film studies have been taught at the University of Nevada, Las Vegas, the university's enrollment has almost doubled, from 5,200 to more than 10,000. The development of film studies here has paralleled the growth of the university. The program has grown from single extension division class to eighteen courses in six departments. Since 1978, the College of Arts and Letters has offered a film studies degree as part of its interdisciplinary degree program.

The Degree Program

The College of Arts and Letters at the University of Nevada, Las Vegas, offers an interdisciplinary degree program. This program allows the student to design his or her own course of study in a well-defined interdisciplinary subject rather than fulfill the requirement lists of a traditional departmental major. Interdisciplinary programs have been proposed in the subjects of film studies, women's studies, Asian studies, British studies, Latin American studies, linguistics, and comparative literature. All matters concerning the student's program, including the appropriateness of the subject and the required coursework, must be approved by the Interdisciplinary Degree Committee. The degree awarded is Bachelor of Arts, and the student's official transcript notes the subject of concentration (for example, "Interdisciplinary Degree: Film Studies").

While the Interdisciplinary Degree Committee might consider an exceptional case, a student ordinarily cannot apply who has accumulated fewer than forty-five or more than seventy-five semester credits (courses each carry three credits). The student must also have maintained a grade point average of 2.5 or better.

While each program is individually tailored, all students must complete a minimum of thirty-six credits in approved courses dealing with the subject of concentration. The student must also fulfill additional credits so that all requirements of both the College of Arts and Letters and the university are satisfied.

Requirements for an Interdisciplinary Degree in Film Studies

The requirements established by the Film Studies Committee reflect the belief that the study of film is at best an interdisciplinary concern. The two required core courses (ENG 194 and FOL 144) constitute Group I and are offered in the departments of English and Foreign Languages, respectively. The Group II courses (film history), of which six credit hours are required, are offered in the Departments of English (ENG 493 and 494), Foreign Langauges (FOL 440, FOL 441/GER 441, and FRE 449), and History (HIS 446).

One production course is required, and the Departments of Art (ART 160 and 460) and Communication Studies (COS 160 and COS 460) offer such courses. The courses dealing with film genres are given by the Departments of English (ENG 495, 496, and 497), Foreign Languages (FOL 443/FRE 443), and Political Science (POS 409a). Three credit hours from this group are required. Three hours of film theory and criticism round out the required course load.

A minimum of twenty-four credit hours of additional film courses out of the thirty-seven hours required for the interdisciplinary degree must be taken. The reading knowledge of a foreign language acceptable to the committee is also required.

Work Cited

Weisstein, Ulrich. *Comparative Literature and Literary Theory: Survey and Introduction.* Bloomington: Indiana Univ. Press, 1973.

Film and Television Courses Offered at the University of Nevada, Las Vegas

FIS 410 (Film Studies): Major Figures in the Cinema   Study of the works of major filmmakers through the auteur theory and other approaches. A different individual will be studied each time the course is offered. (1–3 credits; may be repeated up to 9 credits)

FIS 450: Directed Studies in Film   Individual projects on an aspect of film study, designed by the student in conjunction with a faculty member. (1–3 credits; may be repeated to a maximum of 6 credits)

ART 160: Beginning Art-Film Production   Theoretical examination and practical application of concepts in film. Three hours discussion. Three hours laboratory. (3 credits)

ART 460: Advanced Art-Film Production   Further theoretical examination and practical application of concepts in film. Emphasis on producing a complete work. Three hours discussion. Three hours laboratory. (3 credits)

COS 158 (Communication Studies): Introduction to Broadcasting   A survey of radio and television, focusing on the history and technical aspects of broadcasting, controls on the industry, foreign systems of broadcasting, contemporary programming, and the social impact of electronic media. (3 credits)

COS 160: Television Production   Purposes, scope, methods, and materials for visual and aural broadcasting; planning, organizing, rehearsing, editing, and recording announcements and programs; studio procedures and presentations; preparation of content and form. (3 credits)

COS 460: Advanced Television Production   Comprehensive lecture and laboratory stressing creative aspects of television production. Emphasis on performing and directing broadcast programs. (3 credits)

ENG 194 (English): Introduction to Film   An introduction to the history of international film, film structure and terminology. Survey of the development of cinematic techniques from Edison, Lumière, and Méliès to prevailing contemporary trends, with special emphasis on major directors such as Eisenstein, Ford, Griffith, Lang, Hitchcock, Bergman, and Renoir. (3 credits)

ENG 493: Studies in British Film   A study of the history of British film emphasizing analysis of a variety of films. The student will also examine particular genres, directors, and traditions peculiar to British film and the relationship of British film to England's broader cultural development. (3 credits)

ENG 494: History of the American Film   An examination of the films of major directors fom D. W. Griffith in the Biograph period (1908–12) to contemporary filmmakers. Directors such as John Ford, Howard Hawks, Orson Welles, George Cukor, Robert Flaherty, Frank Capra, Raoul Walsh, and others will be studied. (3 credits)

ENG 495: Film and Literature   A comparative study of the relations of prose, poetry, and drama to the structure and themes of the cinema from Dickens to the present. (3 credits)

ENG 496: The American Hero in Film and Literature   This course traces the origins and development of the American hero from its roots in myth, folklore, and history to the 1950s. (3 credits)

ENG 497: Genre Studies in Film   Individual examinations of genre structures and themes, with emphasis on the development and history of genres. (3 credits)

FOL 144 (Foreign Languages): Language of Film   Introduction to the study of film through lectures, writing, discussions, and viewing of film extracts, with basic film terminology. This specialized course includes shot and analysis in slow motion and readings in the theories of film. (3 credits)

FOL 440: The Continental Film   A survey of the major movements and themes of the European cinema and related literature. (3 credits)

FOL 441 (same as GER 441): Drama and Film of German Expressionism   An examination of German film and literature of the 1910s and 1920s. (3 credits)

FOL 442: Film Theory and Criticism   Specialized course intended for film majors. Major theorists of film are studied intensively with workshop participation in detailed analysis of excerpts and whole films. Special themes will include trends in criticism: political, genre, feminist, etc., with emphasis on structuralism /semiology. (3 credits)

FOL 443 (same as FRE 443): From French Literature to Film   From a cursive analysis of narrative techniques and structure of original literary source toward a detailed study of the basic problems connected with the grammar of film. Students will be expected to read the literary work and/or script if available. (3 credits)

FRE 449 (French): The History of French Film   Survey and evolution of French film from silent to sound: surrealism, realism, and the New Wave. This course will include the work of major filmmakers such as Clair, Renoir, Cocteau, Clouzot, Godard, Truffaut, etc. Films will be analyzed as works of art, social documents, and instruments of communication. (3 credits)

HIS 446 (History): History of the Russian Film   Russian cinema from Eisenstein and Pudovkin to the sentimental realism of contemporary Soviet films, focusing on the interrelationship of ideology, contemporary history, and artistic integrity. (3 credits)

POS 409a (Political Science): Selected Topics and Problems: Politics and the Film   (3 credits)

Creating a Film Studies Program at the University of Manitoba

Eugene P. Walz

Dept. responsible for the film program   English department
Full-time faculty in the intercollegiate dept.   4
Enrollment policies
    maximum class enrollment (if applicable)   "Art of the Film": 50 per section
        upper-level courses: 20
    minimum class enrollment: 10
    average class enrollment   "Art of the Film": 50
        upper-level courses: 18
Staffing
    % of film courses taught by part-time faculty   8%
    % taught by full-time instructors or lecturers   0%
    % taught by asst., assoc., and full-time professors   92%
Program size
    # of students enrolled in the film program in fall of 1981   330
    # of courses offered in the fall term of 1981   5
    # of courses at all levels offered in the program   9 full courses, 5 half courses
    # of students enrolled at the institution   20,000

In retrospect the development of the film studies program at the University of Manitoba can be seen to encompass three distinct phases: a tentative beginning, a period of rapid expansion, and a more recent period of reassessment, consolidation, and more careful design. Like those of most other film curricula in North American colleges and universities, its origins can be traced to the heady expansionism and experimentation of the sixties. Interest in film as an academic pursuit emanated from the Winnipeg Film Society, a large and influential group of people who met regularly to screen European films and American classics that commercial theaters refused to show. Many of the more avid members of the group were employed by the university, and screenings and discussions were frequently held on campus. (Coincidental with the expansion of film studies at the university was the decline into dormancy of the society from which it partly sprang.) Again like many other film programs in North America, film studies got its start here under the aegis of an already established department. In other words, despite the uniqueness of country, province, city, institution, and personnel, the film studies program at the University of Manitoba is fairly typical in its origins, development, and aspirations. A brief description of the history of the program, therefore, might prove instructive to those who wish to develop their own program or change one already in existence.

In 1970, when the Faculty of Arts and Sciences at the University of Manitoba split into two separate entities (each of which now enrolls between 4,500 and 5,000 out of the 20,000 students at the university), a special place was set aside in the new Faculty of Arts for interdisciplinary or cross-disciplinary studies. Here courses such as linguistics, theater, women's studies, Canadian studies, and technology and society could be listed, courses that for one reason or another did not fit comfortably into any of the existing traditional departments. One of the first courses to be proposed and accepted in the cross-disciplinary program was "The History of Film." Although it was an upper-level course, presented without much fanfare, it proved unexpectedly popular with students. This popularity carried over to the course that supplanted "The History of Film," an introductory course entitled "The Art of the Film." While it has undergone many organizational and methodological changes in the past ten years, this course remains the cornerstone of the film studies program.

Both of these courses were drawn up, shepherded through the various curriculum-approval committees, and taught by a member of the English department, a person whose primary responsibilities and interests were theater studies. This was to be crucial in determining the future direction of the film studies program at the University of Manitoba. From the start the film studies program was linked with theater, not so much as one of the performing arts but as an area that was technically staffed and overseen by the English department but outside the mainstream of the department (and, in fact, housed in a separate building on campus). Film studies began as, and continues to be, a satellite program; but it is a satellite that is practically autonomous. A film committee (composed of the people who teach film courses plus two members of the English department) through its chairman handles the design and scheduling of courses, the research and development of new courses and programs, the booking of films, and the dispersal of finances. Weightier matters (hiring and tenure, final approval of courses, etc.) are reserved for the entire English department.

Had film courses been introduced by the School of Fine Arts here, which had been considering a 16mm production course to complement the photography courses it already offered, the program would undoubtedly have taken an entirely different direction, likely emphasizing filmmaking, experimental cinema, and the more "painterly" characteristics of composition and visual/spatial design. Had other departments introduced their own individual film courses, as at some universities, the film studies program would also be completely different. In fact, in the middle 1970s, when only four film courses were on the books, an attempt was made to get interested members of the history, sociology, psychology, religion, art, foreign languages, and computer science departments to restructure existing courses and create new ones that could be aligned with film studies into a more broadly based communications program. Just as the idea was getting beyond the formative stages, however, the person spearheading the operation left to head an already developed communication studies program at another university. As a result, despite the best efforts of a few, the communications program never became a reality.

By 1974 there was still no film studies program as such, merely a series of discrete film courses introduced because of the success of the introductory course, the pedagogic and cinematic interests of the professors teaching this course, and their ability to convince the various university committees of the "relevance" and "academic respectability" (much overused words at the time) of upper-level film courses.

Of the three advanced courses offered, two resulted from the division of the original "History of Film" title into two separate courses, both of which retained the title of the course from which they sprang (evidently to justify their existence as much as to signal their pedagogic intentions)—"The History of Film: Studies in the Director's Cinema" and "The History of Film: The Documentary and Canadian Film." The decision to offer a course that concentrated on directors was an entirely logical one, influenced by the *nouvelle vague*'s "politique des auteurs" and by the English department's traditional emphasis on the work of art as the personal expression of an individual artist. And the importance of nonfiction film in Canada's history makes a course in this subject perfectly justifiable, especially given the nationalistic fervor of the time.

But financial considerations also played a part in the establishment of these courses. During the first years of its existence the director's course focused almost exclusively on directors not associated with the mainstream Hollywood industry whose films were readily and inexpensively available, especially through the Canadian Film Institute's film-lending service (filmmakers like Eisenstein, Welles, Bergman, Godard, and Kurosawa). The "Documentary and Canadian Film" course devoted a good deal of its time to the work of the National Film Board of Canada, whose films could be reserved and shown free of charge through a local office. A third course, "Film Theory and Criticism," was conceived initially as a readings course with a minimum of film rentals. To a degree film studies developed rapidly at the University of Manitoba because the cost of expanding was not as forbidding as it was in some other beginning or expanding areas (computer science, psychology, and others).

With the addition of "Film Theory and Criticism," enough courses were available to prospective film students so that a minor in film studies became feasible. To effect this, the English department committed itself to hiring someone whose training had been in film studies and whose entire responsibility would be film courses. With this double decision a film studies program was begun, implicitly if not officially. Film courses were still being proposed, however, on the basis of personal enthusiasms by people barely aware of what others were doing. A program existed but there was no real coordination or long-range planning. So while courses in experimental cinema and film genres obviously extended the study of film into necessary areas, conflicting courses like "Film Adaptations" (whose course description singled out the cinematic versions of Shakespeare's plays) and "Shakespeare and Film" were being proposed—and accepted—simultaneously. And an ill-fated course in silent films was also introduced. Halfway through its twenty-six-week duration there were fewer than a handful of students left to contemplate the films in the eerily quiet and cavernous screening theater.

It was at this point (in 1975) that the film studies program moved into phase three. The appointment of a new person to coordinate film studies signaled the transition, but a double commitment on the part of the English department actually effected it. First, the department agreed that an expanded, well-balanced program should be developed whose objectives would be a major and ultimately graduate courses in film studies. It was also decided that in order to do this the number of people teaching exclusively in film studies should be increased to four. (One of these four would also teach an introductory theater course.)

Amassing enough evidence to convince the appropriate academic committees, university administrators, the Board of Governors, and the Grants Commission (the body responsible to the provincial government for university funding and management) of the importance of a major forced the film studies staff to reexamine every facet of its program. This was a massive but salutary undertaking. It involved corresponding with other institutions around the world for information about courses offered, objectives, opportunities for students, and opinions on the problems to be anticipated. It also involved canvassing students, other faculty members, high school teachers, and professionals from various related fields (filmmaking, advertising, television, etc.) for advice about tailoring our program to suit the needs of and to utilize the resources in the university and the community.

What emerged from all this was a plan for a program whose aims can be characterized simply as comprehensiveness, coherence, and flexibility. Emphasis would be placed on the narrative structure of film and on the aesthetic and humanistic concerns usually associated with liberal arts education, but other approaches would not be neglected. To accomplish this meant not just adding new courses but dropping some of the existing ones, altering others, instituting half-courses, establishing a logical year-by-year rotation of course offerings, systematically rethinking the various approaches to the introductory "Art of the Film" course, and building a credible collection of books, reference materials, periodicals, and films for the library.

Of prime importance was the immediate correction of previous errors. "Film Adaptations" and "Shakespeare and Film" were both dropped in favor of a "Film and Literature" course that would focus much less attention on the specific debt of some films to print literature and emphasize rather the interrelationships of film and print literature and the common ground of narrativity. "Silent Film" was subsumed into a reconstituted and restructured "History of Film" course that would stress the historical approach to films, not just offer appreciation and analysis of a chronological series of reputable films.

This emphasis on various approaches to film was carried over into the establishment of several half-courses, the film studies program's second priority.

These courses were drawn up to deal with topics that would not lend themselves to extended (twenty-six weeks) investigation. "Popular Film," recently expanded to cover television, examines film as an elaboration of social myths and ideologies and discusses such issues as the star system, violence, and pornography. "Film and Contemporary Consciousness" is the course in which various "isms" and "ologies" have been scrutinized: Marxism, narcissism, feminism, phenomenology, etc. The most serviceable half-courses instituted, two "Special Topics in Film" courses, have given the program the flexibility it needs. Student requests and faculty interests—especially part-time or leave-replacement faculty—can easily be accommodated here. These special topics areas have also served as testing grounds for possible permanent courses. "Film and Contemporary Consciousness" got its start as a special topics course. Screenwriting and basic 16mm production courses are currently being offered there, and in the near future an animation course will be proposed.

The final step in the creation of a film studies program that could sustain a useful and competitive major involved the development of an ideal rotation of upper-level courses in the university timetable. Because every film course could not be offered every year, the following scheme was devised:

Even Years (i.e., 1982–83, 1984–85)		Odd Years (i.e., 1983–84, 1985–86)	
99.223	Film Genres	99.223	Film Genres
99.320	The Director's Cinema	99.320	The Director's Cinema
99.221	The Documentary and Canadian Film	99.224	The Experimental Film
99.227	The American Film	99.226	International Cinema
99.228	Film and Literature	99.324	History of the Cinema
99.325	Special Topics in Film	99.230	The Popular Film
99.229	Film and Contemporary Consciousness	99.327	Film Theory and Criticism

This is for our purposes the ideal paradigm, one that is modified, for instance, to allow for sabbaticals and special circumstances. But it is designed to provide students, and especially majors, an opportunity to choose from a number of different approaches in any given year while at the same time balancing the possibilities year by year. A student interested, for instance, in formal considerations can take documentary film one year and experimental film the next; someone concerned with national issues can alternate "The American Film" with "International Cinema"—which can focus on films from the third world, continental Europe, or Australia in any given year. "Film Genres" and "The Director's Cinema" are offered every year because they continue to be the most popular courses in our program and because different genres and directors are featured each time the courses are offered. In this way a fresh supply of films is virtually guaranteed every year. And students, since they cannot enroll in any course for credit more than once, even though the content changes yearly, are welcome to sit in on screenings for all courses in which they cannot enroll. Thus they are encouraged both to expose themselves to as many different approaches to film as possible and to view as many extracurricular films as they can.

Once the rotation of courses was set in place, the film studies program was in a position not only to apply for the institution of a major but to provide for the various needs and desires of students enrolled in the major and faculty members administering it. Since that time budget constraints have necessitated the suspension of plans to put into place a graduate program. Attention instead has been directed to the improvement of the present undergraduate program, especially the upgrading of the screenwriting and film production courses through the strengthening of ties with a local film production co-op, with a cablevision company that provides air time on the public access channel for student productions, and with the university's theater program.

A major part of our energies in the last few years has gone into overhauling the introductory course, "The Art of the Film." This used to be simply a "great films" course, its organizational principles and even artistic criteria often invisible to an outside observer. Each week a feature film was shown, and the screening would be followed by a lecture or discussion aimed at validating the film's inclusion in the course. Now, although "The Art of the Film" varies somewhat from one instructor to another, it is essentially a two-part course, the first half (approximately) devoted to the formal analysis of narrative films and the second half to broader contexts or frames of reference. In addition, the films are arranged in a rudimentary chronological fashion so that in lectures a basic introduction to film history can also be provided. Various textbooks have been used in the first part of this course: Giannetti's *Understanding Movies*, Bobker's *Elements of Film*, Bordwell and Thompson's *Film Art: An Introduction*, Monaco's *How to Read a Film*, and Jacobs' *The Emergence of Film Art*. No text has proved completely satisfying, though Giannetti's book is most popular with students, while Bordwell and Thompson's probably gets the vote of the faculty—it doesn't have Giannetti's simplifying dogmatism, and it doesn't reduce and fragment things as much as some others. For the second half of the course most sections rely on photocopied handouts and assigned reference materials in the library, but Bill Nichols' *Movies and Methods* and Gerald Mast and Marshall Cohen's *Film Theory and Criticism* have also been used to good advantage.

The first half of my own particular section of the introductory course is further subdivided into three parts: (1) a "backgrounds" or "preliminary considerations" section that relates films to other art forms, especially the visual arts, compares and contrasts narrative cinema with expository (or documentary) cinema, poetic (or "experimental") cinema, and print narrative, and sets out the basic issues to be investigated; (2) a careful exegesis of two short narrative films that can be dealt with as totalities (*An Occurrence at Owl Creek Bridge* and Allan Kroeker's *God Is Not a Fish Inspector* work well because I have access to the scripts and the short stories on which they are based. Fellini's contribution to the anthology *Spirits of the Dead*, "Toby Dammit," and Truffaut's part of *Love at 20*, "Antoine et Colette," have also proved successful); and (3) a systematic analysis of narratve cinema focusing on plot, character, and style. This third section forms the bulk of the term, covering approximately eight of the thirteen weeks.

Over the years I have developed a series of questions (with the help of students and many of my colleagues, past and present) that I photocopy and pass out on the first day of classes and use to provide the basic framework for the first part of the introductory course. These will give some indication of what this course is about.

(1) A movie exists because at every point in its development someone had to make a decision about what to include (and, presumably, exclude). Like other kinds of artists, filmmakers do things and include things because they think or

feel (or simply accept the fact) that these things belong in the film. The basic objectives of this course are to develop an ability to discover and describe WHAT is there and TO WHAT PURPOSE. Although a certain amount of this work will involve separating and isolating factors to be considered, it is important to remember how things relate, how they are bound together to form a coherent work, and how the experience of the film as a whole provides its "meaning."

(2) As an art form of motion, taking place over a period of time, films are a rendering of change. They record a process or a progress. Things must happen, be altered or transformed, grow or diminish in some way. In evaluating the nature of the changes in a film, it is particularly important to notice the opening shots and sequence, the closing shots and sequence, and the transition point(s). What information is presented at the start (before, during, or after the credits) and how is it presented? Is the emphasis on character, action, dialogue, sound, setting? What tensions are established (character v. character, character v. environment, word v. image, etc.)? How are these matters altered in the concluding sequence? Is the resolution at the end temporary or permanent (i.e., is change essential or superficial)? Is the dominant impression at the end one of dynamism or stasis? Have different values emerged?

(3) Plays are built from scenes and acts; films from generally shorter units of shots and sequences that can be orchestrated into larger movements. How is the plot of the film articulated? What are the major sections of the film? How do individual sequences relate to the whole film? What determines the makeup of the individual segments—action, exposition, conflict, surprise, suspense, amusement, etc.? Are divisions the result of changes in location, activity, filmic style, or a character's interior state? What is omitted within and between sequences and to what purpose? What are the predominant structural devices that connect or disconnect sequences or shots (cuts, dissolves, fades to black, wipes)?

(4) What are the major distinguishing features of the principal characters? How do their looks, demeanor, mannerisms, movements, dress, and voice contribute to the impression they make? Are they primarily physical, verbal, or intellectual creatures? What motivates them? Are they active or passive, initiators or responders, moved from within or from outside themselves? Are activities dependent on rigid cause and effect? Do characters assimilate experience, try to control it, or escape from it?

(5) Are there any particular kinds of colors, textures, objects, lighting, or music that are associated with certain characters? What does the positioning of characters vis-à-vis the camera, other characters, or the setting indicate? Do characters seem held in by the frame; do they look past it or break out of it? Is the world on screen an open or closed one? How does a particular location or background help to delineate character or action? When and how do locations or objects take on larger-than-life significance? Can they be said to embody definable values? Is there an evolution or progression in their chronological deployment?

(6) What is the relationship of the camera to the characters, action, and environment (discrete or inquisitive, active or passive, subjective or objective)? Is it consistent throughout, and if not, why not? What causes the camera to move; does it anticipate or follow? What are the reasons for and effects of zooms, pans, cuts from long shots to close-ups, from high angle to low angle, from open forms to closed, from long takes to rapid montage? How do dialogue, voice-over narration, and especially music affect point of view and response?

(7) What challenges do the filmmakers set for themselves and how are they resolved? Are the complexities and subtleties of human experience rendered adequately? In what ways are interior states (emotion and intellection) exteriorized? At what points does action predominate; at what points do character or ideas? As far as can be determined, to what extent does the screenplay (as arrangement and description of incident and creation of dialogue) figure in the overall effect of the film? How about "acting," direction, editing, set design, and music? What issues and elements are avoided and to what effect? Does the film seek to preserve and defend the status quo or criticize it? Is the dominant impression in any way undercut? What does the film make us see (in both senses of this word—sights and insights)? Finally, what is there in the film that confounds or seems to be beyond all of this?

The major part of the first term's activities in the "Art of Film" course involves the application and qualification of these questions to groups of films selected so that analysis of plot can take precedence (but not be the exclusive concern) in the first group of films, character in the second, and style in the third. This part of the course has three written assignments. The first requires that the students provide a sequence-by-sequence account (in abbreviated or point format rather than essay style) of the plot of the film. A brief comment on the overall form of the film is expected—for instance, that *Apocalypse Now* is a quest story or initiation journey up a symbolic river deeper into jungle/darkness/savagery/self. The principal movements in the film must be delineated—for instance, again in *Apocalypse Now*, distinguishing where the introductory exposition ends and what has been accomplished, what each incident (air cavalry charge, tiger discovery, playboy bunny show, sampan shoot-up, bridge attack, and Kurtz's camp) adds to the development of the story and idea of the film. And some preliminary analysis must be attempted—for instance, that incidents in *Apocalypse Now* mark a progress from relative order to absolute chaos, from humorous to horrific incidents, from more sophisticated actions and weapons to more primitive ones, from the realistic to the bizarre and surrealistic and mythic, from light to dark, from an attempt to transform Vietnam into a copy of the United States to an immersion in a primordial past, from being above the world to being submerged in it.

The second assignment focuses on character and requires that students attempt to distinguish as much as is possible between the actor, the character he or she plays, and the performance itself. The assignment is thus divided into three sections: (1) what an actor brings to the role in terms of his or her own physical "equipment," such as general facial features, especially the eyes and mouth, what his or her face expresses naturally, in repose, what his or her range of expressions is, his or her physique, personal mannerisms, gait, behavior, and voice, accent and range; (2) what the character itself is conceived to be, based on his or her occupation, situation, actions, dialogue, his or her growth, development, or lack of such, what he or she thinks of himself or herself and what others think, how he or she compares and contrasts with other characters or actors, and how he or she fits into the mise-en-scène and story; and (3) what the actor's performance does to define the character and affect audience response—for example, how the actor behaves when he or she is first and last seen, how the actor relates to the camera and to what extent blocking determines the impression he or she makes, how he or she relates to groups and setting, what the most demanding physical and emotional moments are and how they are handled, what the movie's climax(es) and/or high point(s) are and how the actor figures in them, and in general what kinds of demands are made.

The third assignment of the first term is the major one and requires that students not only examine a film's plot and characters but also provide a detailed analysis of the style of a particular sequence, mentioning, if relevant, camera placement and movement, lenses and lighting, scenography, color, texture, and composition, editing, sound, and music.

Second-term work revolves on blocks of time devoted to genres, auteurs, and social or theoretical issues with assignments springing from the topics discussed. Students are encouraged to substitute either a storyboard, a slide presentation, or a Super-8 film for at least one of these assignments, depending on the difficulty of the project and the number of students involved (up to three students allowed to collaborate on a movie). Projects are given final approval only after personal consultation, are shown to the entire class, and then discussed as anonymously as possible (unless students wish to be acknowledged). Since my own personal experience as a filmmaker has taught me as much about films and film theory as my academic training, if not more, I try to get as many students as I can to participate in this hands-on film activity.

Much of the second term's work depends on fairly careful coordination of the first-year course and upper-level courses. Genres and directors studied in the "Art of Film" course are taken from films used in the "Film Genres" and "Director's Cinema" courses, and issues discussed in the final weeks of the introductory course often spring from the use of films from other upper-level courses. This coordination provides the program with several opportunities in addition to the obvious one of strengthening the "Art of Film" course: savings on rental fees, the possibility of utilizing guest lectures from upper-level courses to present a different style and approach in the introductory course, a chance to advertise upper-level courses, a point of contrast with the upper-level courses since genres and directors studied on the the introductory level will be different, and a way of preventing the "Art of Film" course from going stale through repetition of the same films year after year.

Perhaps the key to the film studies program at the University of Manitoba, and, I would argue, the key to successful film programs anywhere, is the degree to which the entire operation is well coordinated. Because of the way screening sessions dislocate ordinary academic schedules and because of the intricate planning and expense involved in booking so many films for such diverse courses, a premium is placed on coordinating things in film studies as it is not in any other academic program. (At Manitoba, because the demands are heavy and because no release time is given to the coordinator, the position is filled on a rotating basis.) As a filmmaker I am reminded of just how much in common the head of a film studies program has with an effective film director or producer. Both have to have vision, a gift for dealing with people, and a knack for balancing the theoretical, the aesthetic, the practical, the petty, and the unexpected.

If coordination is the key ingredient in sustaining a film studies program, preplanning is the key to creating and developing one. And this is where the University of Manitoba was somewhat deficient. To continue the filmmaking analogy, the initial script and production schedule were faulty; things have had to be "rescued" on the set and in the editing room. Obviously, then, we cannot propose the preceding outline of the development of the program as a model. Nor do we mean it to indicate that the program has reached a point of static contentment. As we continue to learn many valuable lessons from the experience, we pass it on in this spirit.

Film Studies Courses Offered at the University of Manitoba

99.121: The Art of the Film A survey of the history and aesthetics of the film, from the early innovations of Lumière and Méliès to the present. A critical analysis of the film as an art form reflecting and influencing its society, developed through weekly film viewings, lectures, and discussions. (6 credits)

99.221: The Documentary and Canadian Film Study of the theories and forms of documentary film as an art, as an instrument of social change, and as propaganda. Special emphasis will be laid upon the Canadian documentary tradition and its influence on the Canadian feature film. (6 credits)

99.223: Film Genres An in-depth examination of the history and development of one of the major cinematic genres (the gangster film, the western, the science fiction film, the musical, the comedy, and the mystery or suspense film) and its historic, sociological, psychological, and aesthetic implications. The primary emphasis will be on the permanence and evolution of the generic conventions (setting, characters, action, iconography, and themes) and on the contributions of certain individual directors and stars within these conventions. (6 credits)

99.224: Studies in the Experimental Cinema Cinepoems, expressionism, surrealism, computer and animated films. Formal innovations in avant-garde and underground films and their influence on the feature film industry. (6 credits)

99.226: Studies in International Cinema An examination of film ideas, problems, and techniques from a worldwide perspective, focusing on the contributions of individual countries or groups of countries. (6 credits)

99.227: The American Film The aesthetic development of American film. An investigation of the history of the industry, particular decades or ideological movements, key films and filmmakers, evolving techniques and/or dominant social and intellectual issues relevant to the American film. (6 credits)

99.228: Film and Literature The interrelations between literature and film as revealed through an analysis of significant films, novels, poems, and plays. Special attention to adaptations of Shakespeare, modern drama, the nineteenth-century novel, the modern novel, and popular fiction. (6 credits)

99.229: Film and Contemporary Consciousness Movies as they reveal the life of the mind in the twentieth century. Films of major imaginative and intellectual significance in the light of readings in contemporary psychology, philosophy, science, art, theology, etc. (3 credits)

99.230: The Popular Film Current trends in film as a form of popular culture. Emphasis on recently released films as mirrors of existing social myths and values. (3 credits)

99.320: Studies in Director's Cinema An intensive, critical look at the work of one or two major filmmakers. (6 credits)

99.324: History of the Cinema The development of the cinema from its origins to the diversification of the recent two decades. (6 credits)

99.325: Special Topics in Film I An intensive examination of selected topics in film. Contents of the course will vary according to the needs and interests of students and faculty. (3 credits)

99.326: Special Topics in Film II   (3 credits)

99.327: Film Theory and Criticism   An examinaton of the major theoretical and critical writing in the context of selected films. (3 credits)

Film Study in the Small Liberal Arts College: Carson-Newman College

Jerry Wood

Dept. responsible for the film program	English Department, Humanities Division
Full-time faculty in the dept.	7 (English)
	19 (Humanities)
Enrollment policies	
maximum class enrollment (if applicable)	usually 25
minimum class enrollment	usually none
average class enrollment	20
Staffing	
% of film courses taught by part-time faculty	0%
% taught by full-time instructors or lecturers	0%
% taught by asst., assoc., and full professors	100% (assoc.)
Program size	
# of students enrolled in the film program in fall of 1981	45
# of courses offered in the fall term of 1981	2
# of courses all levels offered in the program	6
# of students enrolled at the institution	1,700

The basic issues of film study are shared by students and teachers in many different kinds of institutions. Whether we are affiliated with large public schools rewarding research and publication or private schools emphasizing quality teaching and long-term commitment to the college, we have at least passing interest in, for example, problems of film authorship, methods of exegesis, and theories of cultural mythology. But in addition to these topics of common interest there are others that often have a special urgency for those of us who teach in small liberal arts colleges. Two of these parochial concerns are pressing these days. The first is a practical one: how to find inexpensive film materials that can be made available for classroom use and intensive study. The second is methodological: how undergraduate film study is to be effectively integrated into the traditional liberal arts curriculum.

Once the teacher in a small college becomes committed to film study, his or her first question often is how to get the "texts." Since private colleges tend to have less adequate funding than do larger, public-supported schools, the answer may at first seem easy—rent the movies the cheapest way you can.[1] But, as in literary study, a second or third "reading" of *The Bicycle Thief* may sensitize the students' responses to the material better than even the most stimulating lectures on Italian neorealism. So the short-term costs of the films need to be compared with the long-term educational goals of the students, teacher, and institution. Eventually the conditions of the rental agreement and the format and quality of the film stock will be as important as the bottom line on an invoice. In fact, most crucial of all may be library and institutional policies on the purchase and holding of films and tapes (called, in the jargon of the trade, software). Even at a Presbyterian college of five hundred students in Ohio, the teacher who initiates a film program most likely will also need to build a film library.

Before making the first purchase for a film library, the instructor will do well to become familiar with the holdings of local and regional libraries as well as those of major universities. Many libraries are increasing their holdings in audio and video equipment as fast as they are adding print materials. Films rented from these public libraries are almost always significantly less expensive than those rented from commercial sources, many films being offered free or for minimal handling costs. Also, the staff are usually extraordinarily supportive of your work. Using libraries does have its disadvantages, however. Many times you must reserve prints months in advance, and films are often full of splices and lines from being mistreated and overused. And, especially in major libraries (like those associated with universities), catalogs (if offered) are hard to use because of the abundance of instructional materials and entertainment films that have to be waded through. When borrowing or renting from libraries, it is helpful to know what you are after and to plan months in advance.

Once familiar with the services of the educational facilities in your region, you can make a systematic survey of film rental companies. Since your funds will be limited, these companies' costs often will be prohibitive because of recent inflation and reduced competition. In any case, be sure to check with these companies about classroom rates and package rates (if you plan to rent a number of films). It is also helpful to make your search with alternate movies in mind, for you are likely to find (as in the case of *Of Mice and Men*) that a print that was available for less than $50 two years ago now runs $200. So start collecting catalogs and programmer's guides to 16mm rental and begin keeping records of the quality of the prints and the service you receive.

If you are able to acquire funds to purchase prints, you will find they cost well in excess of $100, probably more like $400–$500 and up. While some films are certainly worth the investment, you might also give serious consideration to buying from collectors or traders, especially if you find some in your area. These dealers often have good prices on used films, but be sure to have return privileges (in case you get a poor quality print) because the conditions of preowned stock will vary widely.

Especially if you are trying to build a film library in a short time (within a year or two) or if you have a limited budget, an obvious choice would be to investigate the use of videotapes or discs. Even the smallest colleges often have videotape equipment for use in speech, drama, and radio-television courses, and using available "hardware" will reduce your initial cost dramatically. Your secondary costs will also be reduced when you purchase films in tape or disc formats; they are usually about one fifth as expensive as celluloid.[2] In addition to being relatively inexpensive, the tape-disc systems make individualized study and repeated viewings available to your students.

There are also major disadvantages to using other than film stock. The image is not as sharp on tape as film (though discs give a better image than tapes), and the smaller image cools the viewing experience, making a particularly noticeable difference in epics and other films where size (rather than details or depth) is significant. Film teachers using videotapes also need to remember that taping from film results in a smaller image, from which important details can be omitted. An additional problem arises with foreign films. The subtitles are notoriously difficult to read, especially because the image and words are small when played over a monitor. These disadvantages in the use of tapes need to be weighed against two other considerations: (1) tape machines can be used to copy from television for short-term holding (legal questions of *what* and *how long* still must be decided in the courts) and (2) Advent-type projectors, though expensive, can be used to recover some of the experience of the theater.

Using a variety of materials and sources most likely will be your best bet. If you have access to a Super-8mm projector, films from the early silent era can be purchased inexpensively from a number of companies. Later silent and sound films that have been popular enough to be shown regularly on television (which usually reduces demand and thus lowers rental fees) often can be rented at reasonable costs. But motion pictures crucial to the evolution of film as an art form (like *The Birth of a Nation, Citizen Kane, Potemkin,* and *Rules of the Game*), in which visual qualities need accenting by the teacher and review by the students, should be made available in a film library, at least on videotape or disc. Unfortunately, recent major features probably are only affordable at commercial theaters, unless you can tie your film program to campus-wide showings (as in conjunction with a film society).

While acquiring films economically and in a format most suitable for college work is often the major barrier to film study in a small liberal arts college, getting films isn't as chronic a problem as is curriculum development. Like film teachers in larger institutions, the small-college professor will need to justify the teaching of film within a traditional discipline (in my case an English department). But the faculty member in a small school is also likely to be asked to relate film work to the goals of the institution and liberal education in general. Thus, the instructor in a private liberal arts college may feel the need to justify a film program to more colleagues involved in disciplines in no way affiliated with film study than would a peer at a university.

Presenting film study to traditional departments usually begins with important aesthetic issues and ends in campus politics, sometimes trivial and always personal; in one form or another the central question in these academic ad hominem debates is likely to be whether cinema is a form of literature. For those (usually in English or the foreign languages) who would like to see film as an extension of literary studies, the fact that movies and print media both traditionally have emphasized imagery, character development, and the scene is enough to begin analogical discussions of "the literature of film" or "celluloid literature." The repeated and obvious use of literature as a source for filmed stories and the (less obvious) influence of film conventions on literature add some credence to the argument that film should be taught as a form of literature. In a more substantial vein, studies are now revealing how deeply literature and film have shared artistic styles and credos derived from influential movements like expressionism, impressionism, and neorealism. Students of literature thus tend to find a natural affinity between literature and film since the art forms draw heavily from common sources in the theory and methods of narrative art.

But there are clear limits to this kind of comparison making. Movies, even ones that rely on important cues from the sound track, are essentially visual and presentative; literature is verbal and primarily cognitive. Since this literary experience is imagined in the mind of the reader, it is private; motion pictures, on the other hand, usually are shared with others as public rituals. In the most rigorous sense movies may be studied as popular events, but they do not qualify as literature in either aesthetic or social terms.

From such heady issues come the political problems that plague teachers wishing to teach film in any department that emphasizes literary analysis. The expense of films and equipment can be a drain on departmental budgets already sabotaged by the realities of accountability, austerity, and retrenchment. Even when financial objections to film study are answered and the popularity of film courses interpreted as a drawing card for (rather than a threat to) literary studies, movies still can be seen as something other than literature and thus best left to departments of speech and drama or communication arts. The final blow to film study may be struck by faculty members maintaining an elitist approach to the liberal arts; for them, film texts express precisely those values and fantasies from which we should be trying to liberate our students.[3]

It is in response to these financial, aesthetic, and political considerations that I have been restructuring film study at Carson-Newman, a small, private liberal arts college. Developing a film library has been a pleasant task because I have had the enthusiastic encouragement and (better yet) budgeting and clerical support of the head of the Media Services Center. He has helped me find films and tapes, ordered and cataloged the materials, and (more recently) included my requests in his fiscal planning. Through his office I have been able to follow the eclectic approach on purchase and rental that I outlined earlier. The suggestions of my colleagues in the English department, both expressed and implied, also have been useful in curriculum development. Partly in recognition of the real limitations on teaching film study in general, I am now moving toward a primarily cultural approach to film study, in which case film will no longer be the exclusive property of my own (English) department.[4]

In my school, as in most other liberal arts colleges of its size, this means that motion pictures will be studied at the humanities (i.e., divisional) level. In order to suggest the broader base of film studies, I am moving the basic courses ("Introduction to Film Art" and "History of Motion Pictures") from the English department to a general humanities listing. Advanced courses in either director-authors (like Alfred Hitchcock or Ingmar Bergman) or film genres (like the western or horror film) will remain within the English department, where methods of close textual and structural analysis are the usual fare. The major changes will come, however, in the courses that have an explicitly cultural orientation.[5] The course I initiated in the fall of 1980 on the American films of the 1930s and any others I teach as a reflection of a period of American history will be cross-listed in history (in the social science division) and become part of an American studies concentration (still to be developed). Also as a result of this cultural studies orientation, I am beginning a sequence of national cinema courses (historically based and including the French, German, Italian, Soviet, Japanese, and Australian traditions) to be offered in the Department of Foreign Languages. And, although the planning is still in the coffee-room stages, I may teach courses in, for example, humor in the arts and Christian themes in film as offerings of the Departments of Philosophy and Religion. The unifying rationale for all of these changes is that the new wine of cultural perspectives in film study should be put in the old bottles of the traditional departments.

Some of the difficulties raised by this approach are clear to me even before it is well under way. Within my department, English majors who have imagined doing film study for elective hours toward their English major will find fewer film courses offered in English credit. Another consequence of the de-emphasis on film for English majors will be a lower percentage of film students who are well in-formed about the history and methods of cinema study. This new reality will require that I give even more attention to these introductory matters than I have in the past. I also anticipate that a few of my colleagues will see my work as encroaching on their territory and stealing students from their already underattended classes.

But I imagine the advantages will far outweigh these disadvantages. Under the new program the popularity of film will be a drawing card for the whole division, not just for one department. Also, since the Department of Foreign Languages has recently put renewed emphasis on student appreciation of a second culture (as well as language), future film courses will follow the lead of that department. I anticipate that because of this dovetailing of our interests and approaches, teachers in, for example, French, German, and religion will coordinate their literature and culture courses with mine in film. Overall, my work will be less removed from the preparation of my students and the interests of my colleagues.

The most personal advantage of a cultural approach to film is that it encourages my professional growth within the limitations of the liberal arts curriculum. One of the more frustrating characteristics of small schools is their inability to support research; broad-based education leaves little room for courses on such interesting topics as Renoir's American films, Scandinavian influences on the American silent film, or expressionist set design in American films of the Depression. But, given a little nudge now and then, liberal arts colleges can support interdisciplinary courses in Italian neorealism, French literature and cinema, or the American pastoral film, topics that emphasize political ideology, aesthetic theory, or cultural mythology. Intensive study of limited topics is possible, even in the smallest of colleges, as long as the implications are profound and the references broad. In the final analysis, I have created this program because I believe a cultural approach to film study will sharpen the focus of my interdisciplinary interests while I sidestep the narcissism inherent in trying to pursue specialized course work within the undergraduate liberal arts curriculum.

Notes

[1] Larger institutions of course have difficulties funding their film programs, but in smaller colleges, where funds from student activities fees or campus-wide programs are more limited, the very existence of film study is more likely to depend on how the instructor handles film acquisition.

[2] Most tape and disc stores also will rent the films for a day or two for less than five dollars. While rental puts severe time restrictions on use of the tapes, it nevertheless may be the best way to make a number of films available to beginning students.

[3] As if to prove these two contentions, the use of film in departments that do not work primarily with literary texts is showing itself quite successful. In history, movies like *The Birth of a Nation* and *The Seventh Seal* are used to present both realistic imagery from history and the personal and cultural mythology that distorts and interprets history. Documentary and pseudodocumentary films like *Harlan County, U.S.A.* and *The Battle of Culloden* offer visual records of social contexts and politics that can be useful in sociological study. Personal filmmakers who have involvement in, for example, the Christian tradition (like Griffith, Bresson, or Bergman) are often best understood in light of religious questions and ideology.

[4] By cultural study I mean work that is sure to go beyond (without excluding) description of the technical, commercial, and aesthetic factors involved in movie production. Whether the topic is the films of a single director, genre, period, or country in film history, the analysis and discussion put the films in a cultural context. That is, they demonstrate how the films articulate or critique the myths, fears, and ideals—the ideology—familiar to their audience and creators.

[5] Genre and authors topics demand cultural analysis, and even history of film and general introductory courses leave room for cultural perspectives on film.

Proposed Schedule of Film Courses at Carson-Newman College

Fall Semester	Spring Semester	Mini-Term (May)
	1981–82	
American Film Genres: The Western (English)	Film Directors: The Films of Alfred Hitchcock (English)	American Film Genres: The Horror Film (English)
National Cinemas: The French Film (French and humanities)	American Film Genres: The Comic Film (English)	
	1982–83	
National Cinemas: The Australian Film (humanities)	Special Topics: Humor in the Arts and Religion (Religion and English)	American Film Genres: The Western (English)
Introduction to the Art of Film (humanities)	American Film Genres: The Screwball Comedy (English)	

1983–84

National Cinemas:
  The Italian Film
    (Italian and humanities)
Special Topics: Film
  and American Culture:
  The 1930s
    (humanities and
    history)

Film Directors: The Films
  of John Ford
    (English)
American Film Genres:
  The Gangster Film
    (English)

American Film Genres:
  The Musical
    (English)

1984–85

National Cinemas:
  The Soviet Film
    (humanities)*
History of Film
    (humanities)

Special Topics: The
  French New Wave
    (French and humanities)
American Film Genres:
  The Detective Film
    (English)

American Film Genres:
  The Horror Film
    (English)

1985–86

National Cinemas:
  The Japanese Film
    (humanities)*
American Film Genres:
  The Western
    (English)

American Film Genres:
  The Comedy
    (English)
Film Directors: The Films
  of Alfred Hitchcock
    (English)

American Film Genres:
  The Screwball Comedy
    (English)

*These courses are offered for humanities credit because Carson-Newman does not as yet offer courses in the language and literature of the Soviet Union or Japan.

Sample Course: The Movies and American Culture: The 1930s

Primary Texts:
Allen, Frederick Lewis. *Since Yesterday*. 1940; rpt. New York: Harper and Row, 1972.
Bergman, Andrew. *We're in the Money: Depression America and Its Films*. New York: Harper and Row, 1972.

Supplemental Bibliography:
Durgnat, Raymond. *The Crazy Mirror: Hollywood Comedy and the American Image*. New York: Dell, 1972.
Grant, Barry K., ed. *Film Genre: Theory and Criticism*. Metuchen, N.J.: Scarecrow, 1977.
Maland, Charles. *American Visions*. New York: Arno, 1977.
Mast, Gerald. *The Comic Mind*. 2nd ed. Chicago: Univ. of Chicago Press, 1979.
McConnell, Robert J. "The Genesis and Ideology of *Gabriel over the White House*." *Cinema Journal*, Spring 1976, 7–26.
O'Connor, John E., and Martin A. Jackson, eds. *American History/American Film: Interpreting the Hollywood Image*. New York: Ungar, 1979.
Pauly, Thomas H. "*Gone with the Wind* and *Grapes of Wrath* as Hollywood Histories of the Depression." *Journal of Popular Film* 3.3 (1974): 203–18.
Pells, Richard H. *Radical Visions and American Dreams*. New York: Harper and Row, 1974.

Schlesinger, Arthur, Jr. "When the Movies Really Counted." *Show*, April 1963, 77–78, 125.
White, Edward M., ed. *The Pop Culture Tradition*. New York: Norton, 1972.
Wood, Gerald C. "Film and the American Past." Accepted for publication as "The Loss of American Innocence: From *The Clansman* and *Birth of a Nation* to *Gone with the Wind*." In *Making History: Gone with the Wind in American Culture*. Ed. Darden Pyron. Gainesville: Univ. of Florida Press, 1983.

Syllabus:
Week 1: Introduction
Slide Series: *Film: A Reflection of American Values*
Readings: Arthur Schlesinger, Jr., "When the Movies Really Counted."
Week 2: *Little Caesar*
Readings: Allen, 1–81, Bergman, xi–29.
Week 3: *I Am a Fugitive from a Chain Gang*
Readings: Bergman, 30–109.
Week 4: *Duck Soup*
Readings: Gerald Mast, "The Anarchists," in *The Comic Mind*, 281–93, and Raymond Durgnat, "Four against Alienation," in *The Crazy Mirror*, 150–58.
First paper due.
Week 5: *Golddiggers of 1933*
Readings: Allen, 82–171.
Week 6: *King Kong*
Readings: X. J. Kennedy, "Who Killed King Kong?" in *The Pop Culture Tradition*, ed. Edward M. White, 113–17.
Week 7: *Gabriel over the White House*
Readings: Robert J. McConnell, "The Genesis and Ideology of *Gabriel over the White House*," and Bergman, 110–73.
Take-home midterm exam.
Week 8: *The Plow That Broke the Plains* and *The River*
Readings: Allen, 172–276.
Week 9: *Mr. Deeds Goes to Town*
Guest Lecture by Chuck Maland, Department of English, University of Tennessee at Knoxville.
Readings: Introduction and chapter on Frank Capra in Charles Maland, *American Visions*.
Week 10: *Bringing Up Baby*
Readings: Jim Leach, "The Screwball Comedy," in *Film Genre: Theory and Criticism*, ed. Barry K. Grant, 75–89.
Week 11: *Drums along the Mohawk*
Readings: John E. O'Connor, "A Reaffirmation of American Ideals: *Drums along the Mohawk*," in *American History/American Film*, 97–119.
Second paper due.
Week 12: *Gone with the Wind*
Readings: Thomas H. Pauly, "*Gone with the Wind* and *Grapes of Wrath* as Hollywood Histories of the Depression."
Week 13: *Gone with the Wind* (cont.)
Readings: Gerald C. Wood, "Film and the American Past: *Birth of a Nation* and *Gone with the Wind*."
Week 14: *Citizen Kane*
Readings: Richard H. Pells, "From *Little Caesar* to *Citizen Kane*," in *Radical Visions and American Dreams*, 268–91.

Essay Topics:

Essay #1: 1. Choose major national newspaper for your birthday in 1931.

2. Summarize the important national events on that day.

3. Analyze these events in terms of "the times" or the "national character" of Americans.

Essay #2: 1. Choose a major magazine or journal published in the month of your birth for 1939.

2. Summarize its major topics of discussion.

3. Compare with the issues in paper #1 and describe the shifts in American culture since 1931 on the basis of this comparison.

The Film Program at the University of Western Ontario

Seth Feldman

Dept. responsible for the film program	Department of English
Full-time faculty in the dept.	48
Enrollment Policies	
maximum class enrollment (if applicable)	200 (Film 154)
	180 (Film 153)
	90 (Film 153)
minimum class enrollment	N/A
average class enrollment	75 (Film 151)
	200 (Film 154)
	180 (Film 153)
	30 (Film 156)
Staffing	
% of film courses taught by part-time faculty	30%
% taught by full-time instructors or lecturers	0%
% taught by asst., assoc., and full professors	70%
Program size	
# of students enrolled in the film program in fall of 1981	416
# of courses offered in the fall term of 1981	4
# of courses at all levels offered in the program	4
# of students enrolled at the institution	14,000

The film program at the University of Western Ontario is in many ways typical of programs run under the auspices of departments of English. The first film course was approved in 1968, when an unprecedented infusion of funding had transformed the department into one of the largest and most highly regarded departments of English in Canada. Riding the crest of this funding, the course was a freshman-level inquiry into all aspects of film history, aesthetics, criticism, and production. Unlike the department's drama program, which continues to offer courses in all these areas, film at Western is now taught via a set of courses that place their heaviest emphasis on film criticism. References to film history and theory are largely tangential, and there is no program in film production. Nor is there any movement toward an independent film department or film major.[1] Instead, film at Western has taken on three distinct functions: attracting those not majoring in English or arts courses into a critical pursuit, providing English majors with options tangential to literary and dramatic studies, and providing an area into which faculty members may expand their traditional disciplines.

Much of the evolution of the Western program is a direct result of the funding restraints of the 1970s. This is particularly true in regard to staffing the program and to equipping a film production program. Funding the staff required to teach a major (minimum of four full-time equivalents) has become less and less feasible as overall cuts within the department and the university have led to staff reductions. An initial commitment to fund a production program through the university's Media Centre was dissipated as that unit was dissolved and the equipment distributed among Technical Services (the projection staff), the School of Library Sciences, and the visual arts department. Production undertaken at these units has deteriorated to the point where the underused equipment is rented to local independent filmmakers.

In effect, the Western film program has moved from its potential of becoming an independent entity—reflecting a growing interest on campus, locally, and nationally in film—to a limited variant of the pursuits of the English department. The changing position toward the program may be seen in the courses offered and, to a lesser extent, in the manner in which they have been staffed. In its first two years (1968–70), the program consisted of the single freshman course noted above. During the program's third year, the freshman course was divided into two courses on a chronological basis: "Film to 1945" and "Film since 1945." At the same time, the decision was made to offer these courses at the General (intermediate) level (i.e., open only to those who had completed their freshman year).[2] This "upgrading" of the courses had both positive and negative implications. On one hand, it encouraged the program's expansion—as seen in the offering of a third course (a problems course) the next year (1972–73). It also permitted a slightly heavier workload to be given to students within the courses. The move away from the freshman course, however, also served to discourage would-be students and, more seriously, to keep the program from establishing a line of progression from freshman through honors level. Because their designation as film courses separated these courses from the department's other offerings, the possibility of beginning a film major in second year (after taking an introductory English course) was also thwarted, but a remnant of the freshman-level film courses was preserved as a unit of film study within one of the freshman-level English courses.

After the expansion to three courses, the department hired two full-time faculty members to teach film exclusively, a situation that was to continue until 1979 (when budget cuts would force a reduction to a single film specialist). At the same time, faculty members with backgrounds in other areas began teaching film as parts of "teams" in the larger sections. This increased activity led to growing dissatisfaction with the manner in which the courses divided the inquiry into the field. As a way of systematizing film studies, those involved with the program proposed a seven-course rotation, with four courses offered in any given year. The completion of four of these courses would give the student a minor (area of concentration) in film studies. All seven courses would be taught at the General level and thus, again, there would be no attempt to work toward a film major.

The seven-course cycle was approved in 1975 and remains, at least theoretically, the basis for the present film program at Western. In retrospect, the courses adopted seem an uneven amalgamation of individual interests and a desire to cover large areas of the field in a single course. The problems course evolved into the relatively specialized studies of French cinema and film comedy. The course "Film since 1945" thus became limited to postwar, non-American, non-French, non-Canadian works.[3] At the same time, single courses attempted to take in all American sound film, all nonfiction (experimental and documentary) cinema, and all silent cinema. The "Silent Cinema" course was also to incorporate the functions of an introductory course, though it was not to serve as a prerequisite for other courses. It was to be offered each year and was to be the one course required for all those wishing the area of concentration. Finally, in keeping with the department's strong interest in Canadian literature and culture, a course in Canadian film was offered.

The seven-course cycle was taught in 1975-76, 1976-77, and 1977-78, at which time it was reevaluated. It was apparent from the reevaluation that the courses had succeeded in providing the variety of critical approaches that had been hoped for when choosing the various subject headings. The "American Film" course, for instance, had fallen neatly into its intended auteurist vein. It presented and continues to present six to eight directors per year with a relatively short unit at the end of the course covering individual films by a number of more recent artists. Andrew Sarris' *The American Cinema*, the most succinctly stated introduction to the course's critical bias, was chosen as the only required text. When that work was temporarily out of print, Robert Sklar's *Movie-Made America* was used. Students were urged to see the films themselves, to read the texts, to make use of works put on reserve, but not to depend on those outside sources as the bases for their essays.

As might be expected, the auteurist approach used in the "American Film" course was also found to be applicable, at least in part, to some of the other courses. This was particularly true of the courses in film comedy, world cinema, French cinema, and, to a much lesser extent, Canadian cinema. "Film Comedy" succeeded in introducing the concepts of genre criticism—though, as the instructors came to find, the notion of film comedy was less of a genre than an uneasy umbrella for the widely dissimilar aesthetics of silent comedy, American sound comedy, musical comedy, and (the most loosely bonded subset of all) foreign comedy. Texts used included Mast's *The Comic Mind*, Durgnat's *The Crazy Mirror*, and, later, Kaminsky's *Film Genres*. The most attractive aspect of the course has come to be the option of adding a seven-week unit on another genre. The first attempts in this vein—studies of the western and the gangster film—proved to be too condensed to yield the critical coherence intended, but the chronological presentation of seven horror films, from *Nosferatu* to *Night of the Living Dead*, was both intellectually satisfying and enormously popular with students.

The "World Cinema" course and the course in French cinema required the pursuit of questions concerning national cinemas, cinema movements, politics, modernism, and the more recent modes of film criticism. Both courses became the de facto upper-level courses of the film program. Students found themselves working through a good deal of difficult background material supplied as handouts or recommended readings. In the "World Cinema" course, required reading at first consisted of a number of monographs on the individual directors and national cinemas taught. Anthologies such as Mast and Cohen's *Film Theory and Criticism* and Nichols' *Movies and Methods* were chosen less for their relevance to specific films than for the spectrum of critical possibilities they presented. Students were urged to make use of unabridged critical monographs (e.g., Eisenstein's *Film Form*, Bazin's *What Is Cinema?*, Kracauer's *Theory of Film*, the Metz collection, *Film Language*, and Burch's *Theory of Film Practice*). Although Braudy and Dickstein's *Great Film Directors* has come to be the only required text for "World Cinema," none but the dullest students slog through without supplementary reading (this despite our old saw that the films themselves constitute the course text). Similarly, though Armes's *The French Cinema* served as something like a central reference text, a number of studies of individual directors (e.g., Durgnat's *Jean Renoir*, Insdorf's *François Truffaut*, Monaco's *Alain Resnais*) are essential for the "French Cinema" course. "French Cinema" also made use of Milne's translation of *Godard on Godard* both as a study of the growth of New Wave critical thinking and as a guide to the director whose works (eight films in all) formed the largest single unit in the course.

The courses in Canadian and nonfiction cinema were seen as the program's more experimental endeavors. A full year course in Canadian cinema had not, at that time, been mounted. Research was undertaken at the National Film Archives, the National Film Board, and through private distributors in order to select materials. The course became a balance between a historical overview of Canadian cinema (largely the work of the National Film Board) and an auteurist critique of the few major directors (Owen, Shebib, Pearson, Jutra, Lefebvre, Carle) who have appeared in Canada since the rebirth of feature film production in the mid-1960s. The course covered the spectrum of Canadian film activity, including documentary and experimental works. As a result, it came to cover a wide range of problems in film criticism, theory, history, and Canadian culture. During this first year, the course made use of reprints, many of which were later combined with other materials to produce Feldman and Nelson's *Canadian Film Reader* (Toronto: Peter Martin Associates, 1977). When the Canadian Film Institute published its excellent anthology, *Self-Portrait*, that too was added to the course reading list.

The course "Nonfiction Film" was, at first, divided into halves representing both of its pursuits: the documentary and the experimental film. It was later decided to combine the two areas along chronological lines. The intent was to offer a history of these alternative forms of cinema, to provide a chronological orientation for more difficult works, and, when possible, to compare the manner in which similar sensibilities developed in each of the two directions. With the slight exception of two-week units in Brakhage and Flaherty, the course avoided an auteurist approach. Because our students had virtually no experience of cinema other than recent

English-language features, the course attempted to introduce the widest possible variety of these "alternative" materials. The texts available were surprisingly helpful in this regard. In the study of the documentary, Barnouw's *Documentary* and anthologies by Jacobs (*The Documentary Tradition*) and Barsam (*Non-Fiction Film: Theory and Criticism*) proved particularly useful. Sitney's *Visionary Film* and his anthology *Film Culture Reader* were especially apt for the study of the experimental tradition.

In discussing the silent film course, it should be noted that, from an instructor's viewpoint, the course was probably among the most satisfying to organize and teach. Films were (for once) plentiful and quite often as cheap to buy as to rent. The text, Brownlow's *The Parade's Gone By . . .* , is among the most readable film books on the market. The course covered the "primitives," the rise of narrative film, and a wide-ranging group of major directors and individual works. It also made use of documentary and experimental silent film. It thus served its intended purpose of providing a historical and critical introduction to the problems of cinema study. The course's main difficulty was maintaining student interest amid dead silence and untinted prints. As enrollments dwindled the instructors came to appreciate that the acquisition of prints with sound tracks, tints (if possible), and even the occasional banging away on a piano were far more than luxuries.

Reviewing these courses in 1978, those involved in the film program agreed that they had achieved the program's original pedagogical goals. The courses were doing more than luring students into the world of critical discourse. They were an extension of the department's commitment to the creative application of critical theory to new areas. What had been accomplished in applying the mass appreciation of Northrop Frye to areas such as science fiction and children's literature had also been accomplished in film studies. The best evidence of this was the facility with which faculty trained in other areas had enthusiastically adapted their expertise. The program's "converts" had come to include a widely recognized Canadian novelist and expert on the Bloomsbury group, the editor of the complete notebooks and manuscripts of James Joyce, and a prolific 18th-century scholar with an avocation for the writing of detective fiction. Clearly, this was not the deadwood brigade being shipped off to a cinematic Siberia. Rather, they are among the department's liveliest minds and best teachers.

Initially, this divergent group of film teachers sought an intellectual nexus for the program, an introductory text, a glossary, or even a usable bibliography. As the program evolved, this quest became less and less relevant to what was going on in the classroom. Film language and film technique were found to be obscure only to those who profited from that obscurity (i.e., the numerous authors of idiots' guides to film). With minimal bother, intelligent adults could give themselves a useful grounding in film concepts, just as they had previously learned any number of critical subsets. With a bit more bother, excellent introductory lectures were prepared by all concerned. And demystification is contagious. Given this sort of backgrounding and the instructor's patience, students could not only come to "read" films but also look forward to the discussion of increasingly complex works.

This is not to say that the program has dispensed with the idea of an essentially unique filmic sensibility. On the contrary, one faculty member has begun a long-term inquiry into the origins and application of cinematic concepts. In addition, having rejected commercially available material, the film faculty has experimented with its own audiovisual glossaries. These have taken the form of both slide presentations and work with an Athena analytic projector. (The production of a videotaped film glossary is imminent, as it has been for some years.)

Useful as this equipment is in introducing film, its real value lies in its application to specific films as they are presented during the year. The close analysis of a given scene or sequence, the comparison of related compositions, the illustration of points in a uniquely visual manner teach more in a few minutes than do a dozen sanctimonious proclamations from the piles of introductory texts that litter our bookshelves. Indeed, the difference between a student audience watching film as passing entertainment and a student audience studying a film is generated solely by the instructor's commitment to working with the text in this manner.

Let us say, then, that the program at Western represents an application of film studies to texts rather than a systematic effort to further the frontiers of film theory or history. Its pedagogy is dependent entirely upon the films themselves. These are first identified within the spectrum of established critical pursuit. Then they are examined via an observational habit or set of habits that the courses seek to develop. Through rescreenings of entire works or segments of works, students come to find the correspondence between the mode of a given director and the techniques chosen from the pallet of possibilities. In their own writing, students come to realize that what is valued most is a creative understanding of the placement of a work within this spectrum of narrative and technical discourse. Conversely, vacuous generalizations about the meaning of film and regurgitated superficial backgrounding are frowned upon.

Unfortunately, while the courses were successful in evolving this coherent pedagogical outlook, the logistics of mounting them presented the program with a far less sanguine outlook. Those involved in the reevaluation of the cycle noted severe difficulties with student response. A disproportionately large amount of student interest was generated by the American film and film comedy courses. While these courses (with enrollment limits of 180 and 120 students, respectively) were filled and, in one instance, expanded, the courses in world and Canadian cinema reached only one half to two thirds of their enrollment limit of 50 students. The remaining three courses (also with enrollment limits of 50) were less than one-third filled. That this last group included the course on silent cinema—the one course required for the minor—was consistent with the finding that relatively few students were interested in taking four film courses. After some polling of students and student counselors and a discussion of their own observations, those teaching the film courses concluded that these disparities in enrollment were the product of a number of factors. Foremost among these was the tendency of students, particularly students taking an option, to look for familiar material (i.e., English-language narrative film). This was seen to be compounded by the expectation of a certain entertainment value in the courses and, consequently, an impatience with both difficult films and writing assignments. To a lesser extent, the program was being hurt by a student hesitancy toward a commitment to study unknown material in new courses and by problems with timetabling.

The reevaluation led to some modifications in the staging of the courses. With the initial three years of the program behind them, the instructors agreed to design the yearly syllabi around a relatively consistent selection of directors and films. Picking films with which both the instructors and students were comfortable, it was thought, would lead to a reliable set of lectures given to students somewhat familiar with the works (via their colleagues' word of mouth). This was also in keeping with the department's encouragement of annual syllabi modifications not exceeding ten percent of the works taught. By the same token, it was recognized that in a field dealing with contemporary material, some turnover of works would continue.

A more important move was the decision on the part of the department to end the rotation of courses and to offer only the four most popular (i.e., "American Film," "Film Comedy," "The World Film," "The Canadian Film") until such time as enrollment in the program as a whole increased substantially. To cover the large gaps in film studies thus created, the syllabi of three of the four courses were modified. "American Film" came to incorporate at least one silent director as well as at least one silent work by one of the directors regularly studied (e.g., von Sternberg's *Underworld*). "Film Comedy" became "Comedy and Other Genres," including, to date, units on the western and gangster film and a proposed unit on the horror film. The course most changed, however, was "World Cinema from 1945," which came to include units on silent non-American cinema and French film and French directors. It became, in essence, a retrospective of non-American, non-Canadian cinema, a move that solved the problem of accessibility to high-quality prints and served to open up new avenues of inquiry. The course begins with a discussion of four sensibilities as they are expressed by filmmakers: realism (Renoir, Rossellini, Ray), surrealism (Buñuel, Cocteau, Vigo, Fellini), expressionism (Murnau, Lang, Ophuls), and constructivism (Vertov, Eisenstein, Godard). It then presents short retrospectives of the work of major directors (e.g., Bergman, Dreyer, Ozu, Kurosawa) and ends with a five-week unit on modernism in international cinema. This last potpourri touches on the less accessible postwar directors (Resnais, Sembene) and recent developments in emerging or reemerging cinemas (Germany, Hungary, Greece). The structure lends itself to a discussion of the aesthetic options of cinema (the possibilities of style), authorship, and the notion of a national cinema. It allows reference to a wide variety of critics. And it leaves the student with a toehold on current directions in the medium.

Changes were also made in the mechanics of the courses. While the location of the courses within the Department of English prevented a lessening of the writing load for students, it was agreed that assignments would be geared toward easing the burden on the large number of option students who had genuine difficulty with writing critical essays. Instructors would no longer simply ask students to analyze a given film and then depend upon lecture and class discussion to provide sufficient direction for that analysis. Instead, a choice of specific essay topics would be provided for each assignment, each topic relating closely to subject matter covered in class. In addition, more attention was paid to developing writing skills per se. One essay was replaced entirely by a midyear test. At first, these tests were merely one-hour-long identification quizzes, but this format has since been alternated with tests that require answering a question concerning a film screened twice the previous evening or a discussion of a rescreened "sight passage" selected from a previously seen work. The pressure under which these exams were written tended to bring out what had been hoped for in the essays: clear, well-organized discussions of specifics well bolstered by accurate citation. The final exam format—a take-home essay on a surprise film screened three times during the last week of class—was modified only in that the questions were made more pointed and specific. Students were no longer given a slip of paper that said "analyze film X."

Rather, they were presented with a choice of approaches to the film that ranged from an invitation to thematic comparisons to a close reading of a designated passage.

In addressing timetabling difficulties, the film faculty first undertook to lessen the overall number of hours involved in the courses. Students had been asked to attend an evening screening, a two-hour lecture the following morning, a rescreening, and a one-hour tutorial. With the modification, one hour would be taken from the lecture and the second screening was made optional. At the same time, a night section would be offered in one of the two larger courses, while one of the two smaller courses would be taught exclusively in the evening. Both evening courses would be open to both day and extension students. Both would require a screening with a combined lecture-tutorial given the following evening and an optional second screening following immediately after this session. Finally, the timetabling was to be arranged so as to permit a student to take all four courses simultaneously if he or she wished to do so.

During the period 1978–80, the direct and indirect results of these modifications have led to substantial increases in film enrollments. Because both large courses were offered simultaneously, enrollments by day students have improved. In addition, the world cinema course—despite the fact that no one now thinks of it as an automatic B—has doubled its enrollment limit of fifty students, while in the summer of 1980, both the American film and film comedy courses were offered. This response has come despite the fact that screening times necessitate extra class hours during the already intense six-week summer school sessions.

In addition to the development of the film courses, film has come to play an increasing role in other courses within the department and the university. Courses in Canadian literature, science fiction, and Shakespeare all make regular use of film. At the same time, spin-off courses from the program have included an approved (though not yet staged) course on detective film and fiction and a proposed course on film and society. A number of less successful course proposals involving film also attest to a growing interest among faculty members to incorporate what may be seen as a crowd pleaser into their syllabi. This has been true too of faculty in other arts departments who have made use of or plan to make use of the Department of English film facilities.

Many of these associated expansions of film studies as well as genuine qualitative improvements within the program have been made possible by the establishment of a Film and Video Research Center. Essentially, the center comprises a film and videotape collection and the equipment for the viewing, storage, and maintenance of the collection. Films include classics now in the public domain, films bought from distributors, films bought from independent filmmakers, and some videotapes of films not available in Canada. The center was paid for by grants from the university.

The center has had a number of obvious benefits for the film program. The film and video collection and the ready availability of equipment have allowed more flexibility in programming films (for ourselves and other interested parties) and in rescreening works for study purposes. We have been able to acquire films not otherwise available in Canada. Having a film and video collection has allowed those involved in the program to participate in an informal, mutually beneficial exchange system with other universities—thus further expanding the number of titles available to us. The collection has resulted in substantially lowered rental costs. The department, however, has always understood that the variety possible only through a healthy rental budget would be maintained despite the number of acquisitions.

In addition to the facilities of the Film and Video Research Center, funds have been raised for the construction of two optional film-viewing areas. In 1976, again using university funds, the department constructed a twenty-seat screening area for use in film tutorials and by individual researchers. In 1980, the program was granted funds by the university to construct a ninety-seat viewing space for both film and video. The construction of this facility has made it far easier to integrate the showing and analysis of film sequences into lectures. The possibility of using video for this purpose also lessens the wear on films. The new facility has the additional advantage of freeing the program from its dependence upon the university's technical service staff (whose lackadaisical projectionists and patchwork equipment served to undermine the quality of presentations and shorten the life expectancy of the program's prints—all at an exorbitant hourly charge).

If there is a weak spot in the concept of self-contained facilities, it has been the need to hire personnel to organize the use of films, tapes, and equipment. From 1976–78 a full-time media librarian greatly facilitated the running of the center as well as its growth. Attempts since that time to run the center with part-time personnel have been only moderately successful. Not only has the efficiency of the center deteriorated, but the materials and the equipment have suffered unnecessary damage. In 1980 the department secured a grant for a full-time media librarian for the next three years and a commitment from the faculty of arts to fund the librarian after the termination of the grant period.

In summary, then, Western has built up a program and a facility suited to the needs of an undergraduate, intermediate-level survey of the field. There has been very limited student use of film beyond this level (a senior thesis and some peripheral research on a master's thesis). In the immediate future, any expansion will be horizontal (i.e., on the intermediate level) rather than vertical (toward freshman, senior, and graduate-level courses). It may be expected that more courses both within the department and across the university will make use of film. Certainly, more faculty members have become interested in teaching in the area, to the point where the staffing of a fifth course may become a possibility. At the same time, the program will take advantage of the department's experimentation with half-courses by splitting the Canadian film course into two smaller courses (Canadian film and contemporary cinema). The university calendar's sunset law (i.e., that any course not offered during three consecutive years will automatically be dropped from the calendar) may lead to the proposing of replacement courses and a limited reinstitution of the rotation. In addition, new video equipment makes possible the increased incorporation of television studies into the courses—although an entire course in television studies is itself unlikely.

The largest gap in Western's film offerings will continue to be production. The Canadian film course will make some use of video equipment in an exercise aimed at illustrating basic cinema concepts. This will probably take the form of scripting, storyboarding, shooting, and editing a passage from *The Apprenticeship of Duddy Kravitz* and a subsequent comparison of the scene with the version appearing in Ted Kotcheff's film. Students in the world cinema course will be invited to make their own short slide exercises, illustrating a grasp of montage and mise-en-scène. In future years, the relatively sophisticated video tools owned by the faculty of arts language laboratories may open the door to some limited production on an irregular basis. Research is also underway for a long-term proposal to establish an educational software center, a unit within the faculty that would work to encourage the growth of expertise in the production of video-, audio-, and computer-assisted learning tools, but it is unclear at present what part, if any, film students would play in these productions.

Despite these possibilities, video can only dovetail with film production in an extremely limited way. The eventual establishment of an educational software center will not alter the fact that what film equipment there was at Western is irretrievably lost to film students with little hope of replacement. This is doubly tragic given the dramatic expansion of the filmmaking industry in Canada and the expressed desire of the more serious film students to work in production. Given present financial restraints, the best the program will be able to offer its students in this area is a solid critical background and references to other centers.

Notes

[1] In referring to a film major throughout the paper, I will be referring to what would be regarded at Western as an honors degree. Here, and at a few other Canadian universities, undergraduate courses past the freshman level are designated as either general courses—designed either for those pursuing the three-year B.A. or as options—or honors courses, designed for students pursuing the equivalent of a four-year major in the area. Honors courses are generally seen as more difficult, and a student must maintain a B average to remain in the honors program of a given department. Nine honors courses plus the freshman-level second language are required for the department's honors B.A.

[2] See footnote 1.

[3] All of these courses were and continue to be offered on a full-year (twenty-six-week) basis. The departmental policy of offering courses in this manner—and the difficulty of access to major films in Canada—puts an added strain upon the more specialized course offerings.

Film Courses

Film 150: The Silent Cinema   This course is designed to explore the historical and international development of film art from 1896 to 1929. While the relationship of the evolving medium to sociological, political, and historical issues will be examined, the primary focus will be upon the silent film as a mode of aesthetic expression. In addition to lectures and tutorials, there will be a weekly viewing of a film. 1 hour lecture, screening, 1 hour (seminar or tutorial). (Not offered 1980–81.)

Film 151: World Cinema   An introductory examination of the finest achievements of internationally renowned directors, important film movements, and national film cultures. Through screenings and discussion of twenty-five non-American films selected from the entire history of the medium, students develop a means of discussing film as an international art. 1 hour lecture, screening, 1 hour (seminar or tutorial).

Film 152: French Film   A chronological examination of French cinema from its origin to the present. Major directors will be closely studied in the context of historical and theoretical influences. In addition to lectures and tutorials there will be at least one viewing of a film each week. 1 hour lecture, screening, 1 hour (seminar or tutorial).

Film 153: American Film   The development of American film through critical appraisal of major directors' works from both the sound and silent eras. The films examined are representative of their directors as artists and of major social, cultural, and aesthetic movements within the industry and country. 1 hour lecture, screening, 1 hour (seminar or tutorial).

Film 154: Film Comedy and Other Genres   An introduction to the nature and variety of film comedy and other popular film genres such as the musical, the gangster film, the western, science fiction, and the horror film. The twenty-five screenings are selected from the history of the medium. 1 hour lecture, screening, 1 hour (seminar or tutorial).

Film 155: Non-Fictional Film   This course involves examination of two areas of cinema outside the mainstream of narrative features: avant-garde and documentary film. Each area will comprise one term of study. The course will cover the major historical movements of both subjects while exploring the potential of film as a medium of nonfictional expression. In addition to lectures and tutorials, there will be a weekly viewing of a film. 1 hour lecture, screening, 1 hour (seminar or tutorial).

Film 156: Canadian Film   An examination of Canadian film from its origin to the present. The course is designed to acquaint students not only with the growth of our national cinema but also with the various problems attending such development. In addition to lectures and tutorials there will be at least one viewing of a film each week. 1 hour lecture, screening, 1 hour (seminar or tutorial).

1983 Update

Since writing the above description, the enormous growth in film enrollments has led the department to hire a second full-time film instructor. Additional faculty members within the department also teach film courses on a part-time basis. The videotape and slide production exercises have been successfully developed in Film 156 and Film 151. A new video viewing area has been constructed to meet the demand for video rescreenings. As predicted, the university's sunset law has wiped "French Film," "Non-Fictional Film," and "Silent Cinema" from the books. There is a proposal, however, to establish a course entitled "Great Directors," an auteurist study of figures from American and international cinemas. Should this course be offered, "American Film" and, to some extent, "World Cinema" would take on more historical approaches. Meanwhile, for 1983–84, "Canadian Film" has been divided into two half-term (thirteen-week) courses: "Canadian Cinema" and "Contemporary Cinema" (since 1968). This latter course has absorbed some of the titles previously taught in Film 153 and Film 151. Finally, the first master's thesis to make extensive use of film, a study of film adaptations of D. H. Lawrence's works, was defended in 1982.

Salisbury State College was first funded as a teachers college in 1925. The English department concentrated in literature and composition from 1925 to 1962, when, as the current chairman has explained, the "first expansion in related subject matter" came with the addition of linguistics. Folklore was incorporated during the late 1960s, followed by creative writing. Film was added in 1971; journalism was introduced in 1972. All the while the college was being transformed from a teachers college into a liberal arts institution with an extremely open admissions policy. A student body of highly motivated "educationalists" gave way to a more ordinary, career-oriented student body that was not highly motivated. Many of these students brought with them deficiencies in reading and writing. This was not a student population, in short, from which a large number of English majors could be expected.

With the institution of the so-called liberal studies major in 1973 (which enable<sub> students so inclined to escape the foreign language requirement and specific depart mental course requirements as well), the number of English majors dropped significantly; while the student body doubled to over 3,500 by 1981, the number of English majors dropped from nearly one hundred to approximately fifty. Popular English courses—American literature, the short story, folklore, and several film courses, for example—tended to fill with liberal studies majors, some of whom in former times surely would have become English majors. Other potential majors were lost to a newly formed communication arts department. During that same period the number of English department faculty members increased from nine to about fifteen. The department has recently established a flexible program for English majors that will enable students to "concentrate" in film, folklore, linguistics, journalism, or creative writing and enable some majors to escape the foreign language requirement to which majors in no other department at this college have to submit; perhaps this will enable the English department to replenish its population of majors.

The change that has taken place in the department in 1981 will later be explained in some detail. It was, I believe, a natural consequence of the expansion of the college and the extended and diversified frontiers that came with the department's growth. Defining the role of cinema, that "fabulous newborn progeny of the Machine and Feeling," as Ricciotto Canudo described it in his "Manifesto of the Seven Arts" in 1911, was no easy task. How does one place, departmentally, a "total art towards which," as Canudo asserted, all "the other arts, since the beginning, have always tended" (253)?

Although its genesis stretches back no more than eighty-odd years, cinema—serious cinema—has certainly come to be regarded as a full-fledged art form. Its history and theory will be examined by specialists in cinema studies departments of large universities, but its substance, its content, should also reasonably be studied as a respected branch of the humanities. In the premier issue of *Literature/Film Quarterly*, Edward L. Ruhe suggested that "in the philological spirit English departments are traditionally protective of orphan and fledgling disciplines" and that "sizable English departments maintain a kind of frontier where new disciplines of humane promise can be tested" (78). Small colleges lacking cinema studies departments need not be deprived of the privilege of dealing with cinema as a worthwhile and valid expression of humanistic study. Cinema courses can be and are being taught by departments of English and foreign languages, both at small colleges such as Salisbury State and at large, technologically oriented institutions such as

The Film Program at Salisbury State College

James Michael Welsh

Dept. responsible for the film program	Department of English
Full-time faculty in the dept.	15
Enrollment policies	
maximum class enrollment (if applicable)	75
minimum class enrollment	10
average class enrollment	45
Staffing	
% of film courses taught by part-time faculty	0%
% taught by full-time instructors or lecturers	0%
% taught by asst., assoc., and full professors	100%
Program size	
# of students enrolled in the film program in fall of 1981	6*
# of courses offered in the fall term of 1981	3
# of courses at all levels offered in the program	15
# of students enrolled at the institution	3,500

*The film concentration program in the English department was initiated, proposed, and approved by the department and college during academic year 1979–80. Though film courses have been offered for the past ten years, there was no specific program in operation in the fall of 1979. The film concentration was not put in place until academic year 1981–82, with initially six students expressing interest in the new program. In the near future we intend to publicize this concentration actively on campus, since it should have obvious appeal for majors in the two participating departments, English and communication arts.